Jonathan Mc

Jonathan is an actor, writer and c
leading roles on stage (Royal Shakespeare Co., Royal Court
Theatre, Chichester Festival, Royal Exchange Theatre),
television and radio. He has directed plays and music theatre
world premieres (English National Opera, Scottish Opera, BBC
TV, Munich, Venice, Barbados etc.)

His plays include:

Street Captives (Edinburgh Festival/Royal Exchange Theatre
/Gate Theatre) *Obstruct the Doors, Cause Delay and Be
Dangerous* (Cockpit Theatre) *Treatment* (Edinburgh Fringe
First Award /Donmar Warehouse and performances worldwide
/BBC Film starring Jonathan Moore and Gabriel Byrne), *Behind
Heaven* (Royal Exchange Theatre/Donmar Warehouse),
Regeneration (Half Moon Theatre) *This Other Eden* (Runner-
up Verity Bargate Award, Soho Theatre Co.) *Fall From Light*
(Royal Exchange Theatre commission)

Text for music theatre:

Adapted and directed *Greek,* from the play by Steven Berkoff,
music by Mark Antony Turnage (Munich Biennale/Best Libretto
Award), (Edinburgh International Festival and English National
Opera at the Coliseum/Olivier Award Nomination) *Horse Opera*
(Channel 4 film, music by Stewart Copeland) *East and West,*
text and direction (Almeida Theatre, music by Ian McQueen),
Mottke the Thief, text and direction, (Bonn Opera, music by
Bernd Franke).

'Moore tackles relationships, religion and violence head on.'
New Musical Express

'*Treatment* is one of the most vibrant and astonishingly truthful pieces of theatre to have emerged in recent years. Moore writes and performs with passion and intensity and possesses an extraordinary mature talent.'

Drama Magazine

'Watching this play, I had some idea what a sense of discovery spectators must have had that May night in 1956 when 'Look Back in Anger' exploded onto stage...'

Boston Phoenix

'Deals with the raw violence of street-fighters with a starkness and purity seldom encountered in the theatre. A daring and poetic use of language.'

Time Out Magazine

'This explosive drama which rocks... with its violence and energy...'

The Independent

'Moore's artistry lies in the delicate weave of realism and ritual... At home with both the male and female sensibility, Moore weaves magic.'

Toronto Globe and Mail

'For the first time on TV – fact or fiction – here is a drama which enables us to take a glimpse inside the mind and morality of football fans... remarkable, sharp and frightening.'

The Daily Express

'The most exciting piece of theatre now in town.'

Toronto Now Magazine

'Moore's Miracle Treatment!'

London Evening Standard

'Theatre at its best!'

Financial Times

Three Plays

Jonathan Moore

Treatment

This Other Eden

Fall From Light

AURORA METRO PRESS

Trade distribution:
UK - Central Books Tel: 020 8986 4854 Fax: 020 8533 5821
USA - Theatre Communications Group, N.Y. Tel: 212 697 5230
Canada – Canada Playwrights Press Tel: 416 703 0201

ISBN 0-9536757-2-6   Printed by Antony Rowe, Chippenham, UK.

*Dedicated with love and thanks to Nora and Richard,
my Mum and Dad, and to the Creator of all people
of all religions, all cultures.*

Contents

Introduction by Gregory Hersov　　　8

Treatment　　　12

This Other Eden　　　59

Fall From Light　　　115

Introduction
Gregory Hersov

So, England in the 1980's. The Dawning of Thatcherism. A time of fundamental change. The total devotion to free enterprise and the free market. A relentless attack on socialism as an outmoded way of living. A questioning of there being such a thing as society. A time of conflict, violence, anger. Whatever happened is still happening into the 21st century despite the modernisation of New Labour. Changes were made and growing up in this country in the shadow of Thatcherism, produced a new culture and new voices.

What happened to the British theatre? The New Wave of the 1950's – Osborne, Pinter, Arden *et al* had completely rearranged what could take place and whose experience could be represented on the stage. The tone of their writing was strong and abrasive, they consciously wanted Theatre to *not* be the preserve of a cosy middle-class that simply wanted their lifestyle validated on a night out to the theatre.

In the late 1960's and 70's, the public, radical epic theatre of Brenton, Barker, Hare, Churchill *et al* continued the path of change. The theatre became a place where the state of the nation was dissected and criticised. The whole history of the country was looked at with a new critical gaze. Established ideas were undercut. The hope for a political change from the left permeated the work. British Theatre was consistently progressive. State funding for the arts was seen as essential to the spiritual health of the country. More theatres were built and more plays were seen throughout the land. But in the 1980's, Thatcherism saw the theatre as a threat. Experimentation, imagination, political attitude were pushed aside as market forces, corporate techniques and the new managerial culture ruled. Value for money became the main criteria for funding. The theatre was in retreat and playwrights had to toe the line. The right to be creative, questioning, radical was no longer a given.

RILLINGS... But now. Now it's different. It is. The soul's gone. Some... dead soul, some great big dead soul's sitting on this country. No values. No love. Junk food. Junk minds. Junk hearts. Sorry...

(Fall From Light)

Jonathan Moore is an actor, director, librettist, opera regisseur and playwright who has been one of the few distinctive, passionate and original voices in England over the last twenty years. His theatre is a place of confrontation, violence, class-conflict that disturbs and provokes. But his plays also contain a real exploration of transcendence, the nature of love, the nature of spirituality and the need for union. The juxtaposition of these two impulses saturate all his work and coupled with a love of language and stylistic innovation makes his plays brand themselves into our consciousness.

RORY Take a look at me, right? What do you reckon you're seeing? Yeah. Me. I'm here. I ain't dead.

(Treatment)

Class is alive, *alive-ho* in these plays. Moore refuses to accept that class has disappeared, that we live in a classless society, that there's no division, hierarchy or conflict between the classes in this country (one of the central ideologies of Thatcherism). These plays are fuelled with anger and fury on the part of many of his characters – Liam, Rory, Dave, Girly and his gang – at how this country sees them, represses them, ignores them. These characters go into battle for their identity, they terrorise their betters, they are frustrated and angry at being written off from birth. They prove themselves to be cleverer, wittier, more curious and more passionate about life and its possibilities than their so-called superiors. They refuse to be passive or dead. They've been created to scare you if you're unthinking about what it means to be privileged, they're there to represent you if you feel disempowered and useless. And yet violence, (which happens in all these plays) isn't the way forward. It happens but it's never what the characters really want. They're looking for something else.

DAVE   How Irish am I Mum, anyway? Am I English? Irish? What?
HANNAH   How do you feel?
DAVE   I dunno.

(This Other Eden)

Moore's Irish roots are crucial to his work. *This Other Eden* explores this split in identity. Irishness is seen as a complex series of ideas, feelings, aspirations. A love of language, a wish to transcend, a need for earthly and heavenly love. Whatever is going on in a Jonathan Moore play, this yearning for wholeness, this quest for 'A directed energy. Applied. A noble soul' underlies all his characters. Ireland is a different culture both poetic and political, an articulate, generous, warm attitude to the people one loves or tries to love. Hannah returns there literally at the end of *This Other Eden*. Liam and Rory stay in England, Rory beats up Father Michael but the struggle and the conflict between anger and love never ends in *Treatment*. Moore's intense romanticism in the way he writes relationships, as well as the strength and courage of his female characters, who are often charting a different way through life from his male ones, come from his sense of history and identification with the Celtic Other, alien to the England he lives in.

MR SMITH   I've had vole milk shake.
SHRIMPDICK   You fuckin' liar.
VELVETBLADE   No one's had vole milk shake.
MR SMITH   I have. Same thing. Blender job.
VELVETBLADE   Alright. What'd it taste like then?

MR SMITH Unusual really. Sort of nutty, woody, with a trace of smoke and yet with a certain –

SHRIMPDICK You tossy liar, you know what I mean?

MR SMITH I ain't. There's no taste quite like vole.

VELVETBLADE Oh shut it will ya or I'll put your knob in a blender.

MR SMITH Look if you had a choice of my Keeley's cooking or a glass of vole milkshake you'd be going, "Gimme the vole, gimme the vole."

(Fall From Light)

Oh yes, Moore's plays are fun too. His characters speak in the highly direct language of the street. They also take off into flights of fancy and lyricism with images falling over each other to reach you. His language is crammed with references to film, jazz, opera, punk, TV sitcoms, tabloid headlines, great philosophical works. *A Clockwork Orange* to *On the Buses.* Beethoven through to Henze ending with Tammy Wynette. No distinctions between high and low in these plays. In fact, *Fall From Light* is a whole plethora of art forms reflecting the emotional battles of the characters. A prosaic naturalistic theatre is death. These plays are fragmented collages: monologues with invading dialogues, music propelled rhythmic chants and alarming physical and visual images. You never know what's going to come next but the whole of late 20th century cultural energy rips through these pages.

Treatment was written in 1981. *Fall From Light* in 2001. Over 20 years Moore has written a wide range of work that does stand up and say what it has been like living in England. Whatever he does as a writer, actor, director in theatre, opera or film, he makes art that is never trivial but always searching and confronting the big things that face us every day of our lives in this difficult world we inhabit.

Gregory Hersov is Joint Artistic Director of the Royal Exchange Theatre, Manchester. He directed another of Moore's plays, *Behind Heaven.*

Treatment

When I first directed this play on the Edinburgh Fringe, something strange happened. Something mysterious and magical and almost beyond our control. We felt we had tapped into a spirit, a feel of the age, very specific to its time. Audiences were shocked, stunned, cheering and weeping. People still tell me how much those performances affected them.

Since then, there have been many productions of *Treatment* both professional and amateur, most notably at The Gate, The Donmar and for BBC Television. I saw the play again recently at The Finborough Theatre in London, directed by Jacob Murray and produced by Clarissa Young for *State of Unrest* Theatre Company. It showed me that a new generation could make this play their own.

I'd like to thank the following for their inspiration and commitment to the early productions of the play: Steve Brown, Michael Kingsbury, Ros Goldsmith, Roger Monk, Bryan Oliver, Souad Faress, Katrin Cartlidge, Terence Wilton, Jonathan Stratt. And those involved with the BBC TV film version, directed by Chris Menaul: Gabriel Byrne, Peter Macnamara, Suzanne Crowley.

Jonathan Moore

Treatment

CHARACTERS
Father Michael
Liam
Rory
Julia

Setting: London   *Time:* The present

Performance Note:
The style of this play in performance should be disciplined, physical, poetic, ritualistic. It should be a stylistic contrast between naturalism and heightened ritual. A mimimum of props and sets is best, performed with a maximum of physical and emotional commitment.

SCENE 1
Darkness. Lights up on Father Michael alone.

F. MICHAEL I didn't plan anything. Just a freak. The joining together of bread and water. A quiet drink. The real sound of pouring liquid. I'd rather be anywhere else than here. That's not true. A partial gravitation motion. A gradation. A thought flow. Nothing too strenuous. However it wasn't that easy. Or that simple. In fact it was probably the most difficult thing to be involved in. With. Scientific? Perhaps. Emotion? Certainly. Einstein's skeleton must be very old by now.
Sun thoughts. Thoughts from abroad. Clarity of ignorance. That sort of thing. The usual extraordinary. The peacetime

blues. Darkest Africa. That could have been the place.
Or India. Any colony. Brushstrokes. Sound and colour.
Blessings from Fathers in foreign lands. The whole
landscape of thought. Of course it needn't have been so
linear. A short burst of ecstatic need would have been
enough, but time was on their side. Thankfully these
considerations bless the paucity of originality.
Moondust. Thought and plague. It could go anywhere.
The music started. Tuning instruments. A concert hall.
Endless tuning. The music started. Suddenly I was there.
It blessed me. The flavour of freshness, bathing the skin of
the soul in textured eternity. Heed me. Hear this. The
certain knowledge of the tragic never fails me. Constant
brushes with the daemon, existing endless battles with the
vessel. Will the vessel stand up to the pressure of the force
passing through it? Atavistic? Possibly. Certain? Yes. It is
always with us. I feel the force passing through specially
chosen, sometimes exceptionally fragile vessels of
creativity, daily. All over the world. Think about it. Think. A
truly wonderful thought. As natural as the sun. Simple. Full.
I do battle with myself, the fragile container of this need.
The all powerful shaper of creation.

Blackout.
Spotlight on Liam.

LIAM   O Death where is thy victory?
                 O Grave where is thy sting?

Blackout.
Spotlight on Rory.

RORY   Take me right. Down the Bridge on a Saturday
afternoon. Fucking head case. Trim lined footwork. Blues
on the loose. Blades out.

Blackout.
Lights up.

RORY Seen the price of a season ticket?
LIAM Gotta be rich mate.
RORY Or smart, like us.

Blackout.
Lights up.

RORY It can be any type of gear. Speed. weed. We
get up and out on it, Flash the ash.
LIAM On your bike, mate.
RORY Ash.

Blackout.
Two spotlights. Father Michael in one, Liam kneeling in the other.

F. MICHAEL A life of crime liberates one from the ordinary.
It makes a personal statement of emotional liberty. I find it
challenging, refreshing. Blessings, age old and pre-
Reformation, Old Testament and Michelangelesque.
Flared nostrils attending Palestrina in the Cistine Chapel.
Our own personal glory. A translation of the glory of death.
Why not? A new movement. Terror pianos of guilt.
Striving with the current. How can these multifarious
images be enjoyed? Through death? Guilt? I feel nothing.
I feel all. Look at me. Eccentric figure. The court jester of
retribution. The drunken porter at the gates of Heaven.
The herald of death with a clown's mask. You are holy. I
bless you and ask you to bless me. I do not contravene
your sacred love. I do not risk to question your love. The
nature of your complete hell.
LIAM I never ask for nothing. Nothing. I am nothing.

F. MICHAEL Your purity refreshes me. I am refreshed. I see you as a desperate revenger in the grand tradition. I despise nothing. I see you as an open receptacle. A vessel for goodness. The daemon. Powerful full throttle engines pushing the force in on itself. Nature never moves that quickly. History categorises, love unites.

LIAM   'Out of the depths, I cry to thee O Lord
Lord hear my voice
Let thine ears be attentive
To the voice of my supplication'

Blackout.
Lights up on Liam and Julia.

JULIA *(post coital)* Why don't you trust me?
LIAM   Do what?
JULIA   I love you.
LIAM   It ain't right. Ain't healthy.

Blackout.
Lights up on Julia alone.

JULIA   He never responds fully. He is terrific. Awful. I despise his ignorance. Love his body. His body. He has no real strength. I tower above him. I hate myself for it. He needs me in his weakness. I respond to that. It's so complete. So totally satisfying. It's easy to laugh. I laugh at him. He's a child. A worthless child. I love him.

Blackout. In the darkness, a drum beat.
Lights up. Liam and Rory. Jagged electric guitar joins in.
White noise. Loud.
Mime fight: *The two boys walking along an underpass, staring at the audience. The audience is made to feel like an on-coming pedestrian, caught in the underpass. Flashing light*

in time with the music – a pulse effect also suggesting a defective, flickering fluorescent light. The boys faces contort in exaggerated delight as in slow motion they mime the beating up of the on-coming pedestrian. Their movements are flowing, passionate, but controlled. Their legs move back as the invisible victim hits the floor. Lights change. The boys now savagely kick the victim in real motion. They both sprint to the front of the stage, left and right, hands in the air, triumphant, screaming.

LIAM/RORY *(To the tune of: 'When The Saints Go Marching In*)*

Oh When The Blues
(Oh When The Blues)
Go Steamin' In
(Go Steamin' In)
Oh When The Blues Go Steamin' In
I Wanna Be In That Bundle
Oh When The Blues Go Steamin' In
(Repeat once, then:)
CHELSEA! CHELSEA! CHELSEA!

Lights change. Naturalistic.

RORY	Three fucking nil. Amazing.
LIAM	Yeah.
RORY	You seeing that bird tonight?
LIAM	Too right.
RORY	What's the time?
LIAM	Half five.
RORY	Goin' down the boozer. You coming?
LIAM	Nah.

---

*Or update to the football songs of the day.

RORY   Don't be a prat. What's the matter? You ill? Overdid it on that Paki geezer, you reckon? Bet he won't come down Stamford Bridge too often again.

LIAM   Yeah.

RORY   They eat dog shit.

LIAM   Who?

RORY   Them Pakis.

LIAM   How d'you know?

RORY   I seen 'em do it. That geezer in 56. He comes out of his house. Looks round him, conspicuous like. He never sees me coming. He bends down, licks his lips and tucks in. Burped afterwards.

LIAM   You bleedin' liar.

RORY   On my life. I had to teach him a lesson. Mind you, they ain't as bad as them geezers down Arndale Estate. You missed ruck last Friday didn't ya? About twenty handed we was. They was fuckin' mob handed. Well, we steamed in right, and I'm in there with some Turkish bastard or something, crunching his bollocks with me boots, when this big gorilla grabs me from behind. 'Right, you Chelsea wanker,' he goes, 'You're dead.' So he only gets out this blade, don't he? Some of us went in tooled up. But I had mine kicked out of me hand by the Turk. I fuckin' elbowed him in his guts, scraped his shins with the back of me boots. I span round, held his tooled up hand, nutted him. The prat goes down, don't he? So I've had his tool and I'm laughing me head off. 'OK fat arse, here we go.' I only lopped his bleedin' ear half off, didn't I? He's going: 'You bastard, I know where you live. And that bleedin' brother of yours.' 'Oh yeah?' I goes, 'You lay one finger on me brother and you'll be a soprano, sunshine.' Then I slashed just above his wedding tackle with the tool and we all pissed off. *(Beat.)* Might see you down the pub then?

Rory exits.

Lights change. Music. Liam and Julia lie together.

JULIA   I could go anywhere. From here. After
     Cambridge it seemed pointless to get away.
LIAM   Want a fag?
JULIA   Thanks. You're beautiful, do you know that?
LIAM   Beautiful? How d'you mean?
JULIA   Like a god. A statue. A renaissance hero.
LIAM   Cheers. You ain't too bad yourself.

Blackout. Music.
Lights up. <u>Father Michael's study.</u> Father Michael alone.
Liam enters.

LIAM   Hello. Do you mind?
F. MICHAEL Certainly not.
LIAM   I was in the church. I wanted to talk to
     someone.
F. MICHAEL Of course. Please sit down. *(Liam sits.)*
LIAM   Ta.
F. MICHAEL Well?
LIAM   I er – I wanted to have a chat, sort of thing.
F. MICHAEL What about...? Go ahead.
LIAM   I used to come regular. With me family.
     I stopped coming though.
F. MICHAEL Why's that?
LIAM   Dunno.
F. MICHAEL I see.
LIAM   It's quiet. I like the smell. I like it. You're new
     ain't ya?
F. MICHAEL Yes, I am new. Well, I've been here a year now.
LIAM   Oh. *(pause)* I'm sorry I shouldn't have come.

F. MICHAEL Of course you should. I'm glad you dropped in. Where are you from?

LIAM   Highshaw Estate.

F. MICHAEL I know it. I have a lot of friends from Highshaw.

Pause.

LIAM   You ain't old are you?

F. MICHAEL I don't think so.

LIAM   Most Priests are old.

F. MICHAEL I don't know about that one. What's your name?

LIAM *(mumbles)* Secret Squirrel.

F. MICHAEL I beg your pardon?

LIAM   Top Cat.

F. MICHAEL Ah. One of my favourites. I like the theme tune.

LIAM   'The indisputable leader of the gang.'

F. MICHAEL That's right.

LIAM   Do you like me?

F. MICHAEL Of course.

LIAM   Why?

F. MICHAEL You seem like a nice person.

LIAM   You're having me on. I thought priests weren't supposed to lie?

F. MICHAEL It's the truth. I like you. Top Cat.

LIAM *(laughing)* Top Cat. That ain't my name.

F. MICHAEL Maybe not. But I like it.

LIAM   Don't you want to know my real name?

F. MICHAEL Not necessarily. Not if you don't want to tell me.

LIAM   Who said I never?

F. MICHAEL Alright, what's your name?

LIAM   Ain't telling.

F. MICHAEL Ain't telling. Interesting. Is it Greek?

LIAM Do I look like a Greco? Thanks a lot.

F. MICHAEL It could be a compliment. *(pause)* Why did you come to see me?

LIAM I needed to talk Father.

F. MICHAEL Of course. What about?

LIAM *(staring, intense)* In there. On me own. Blackness. It's dark and it smells like people dying all round the world. Like Chelsea on a Saturday. That's what it smells like. Earth. Turfy, know what I mean? Incense and altar cloth. Then you sit down. On your own. Your head on your body, like your body ain't there or something. Know what I mean?

F. MICHAEL I think so.

LIAM Feels like speed an' all.

F. MICHAEL Really?

LIAM Done a lot of that I have.

F. MICHAEL What?

LIAM Speed.

F. MICHAEL Sorry?

LIAM I snort it. Used to. Don't no more though. You shocked Father?

F. MICHAEL Not really. Should I be?

LIAM I like you.

F. MICHAEL Thank you.

LIAM I was lying. I hate you.

Pause.

F. MICHAEL What's the matter?

LIAM Nothing. I'm OK.

F. MICHAEL You wanted to talk to me. Can I help?

LIAM No. I just felt like coming in. I walked through the pass door from the church. I was bored. Just felt like it.

F. MICHAEL That's fine by me.

LIAM   Ain't you scared?

F. MICHAEL No.

LIAM   Bet you are. Scared shitless.

F. MICHAEL I'm not. really.

LIAM   Well, you should be. You should be terrified, mate. I might have come here to do you.

F. MICHAEL Do me?

LIAM   Have your money away. Do the place over. *(pause)* I bolted the door on me way in. Now you scared?

F. MICHAEL Do you want me to be scared?

LIAM   Ain't bothered. *(pause)* You ain't half boring. Can't you say nothing funny?

F. MICHAEL Not really.

LIAM   Watch this. *(He turns a cartwheel)* What d'you think?

F. MICHAEL That's very good.

LIAM   Bet you can't do it.

F. MICHAEL I shouldn't think so.

LIAM *(screaming)* You can't do fuck all, can you?

Pause.

F. MICHAEL Listen, just calm down. Sit down and we'll have a chat.

LIAM   What?

F. MICHAEL We'll talk. That's why you came here wasn't it?

LIAM   Oh yeah. Sorry.

F. MICHAEL Sit down. *(Liam sits.)* That's better. Feeling better?

LIAM   Yeah. A bit.

F. MICHAEL Now let's have that chat shall we?

LIAM   Go on then.

Pause.

F. MICHAEL Well, are you still at school?
LIAM   Nah.
F. MICHAEL Work?
LIAM   Nah. *(pause)* Is that all? Can I go now?
F. MICHAEL If you like. *(Liam gets up and walks away.)* Do
you want to leave your address?
LIAM *(suddenly screaming)* Oh, I see! You want to report me
to the filth, you sly sod. Why do you lot always do the dirty,
you fucking posh shits? I hate you. *(He smashes a chair.)*
F. MICHAEL You needn't leave your address. Not if you
don't want to. It's just that I'd like to see you again. I
would.
LIAM   Why?
F. MICHAEL I've told you. I like you.
LIAM *(calm)* You'll go to Hell you will. All these lies.
F. MICHAEL Will you tell me what your name is?
LIAM   Why?
F. MICHAEL I'd like to know.
LIAM   That's for me to know and you to find out.

Pause.

F. MICHAEL I see.
LIAM   What's your name?
F. MICHAEL Michael.
LIAM   Father Michael?
F. MICHAEL If you like.
LIAM   Well, I don't mind.

Pause.

F. MICHAEL How long have you lived on Highshaw?

LIAM   Fifty years. *(pause)* Where were you before you came here?

F. MICHAEL Yorkshire. Do you know it?

LIAM   No, never been abroad. *(pause)* What's it like?

F. MICHAEL Pardon?

LIAM   Being a priest.

F. MICHAEL Oh dear, that's a tricky one.

LIAM   Do you like it?

F. MICHAEL Well – yes. Of course. I love it. It's hard sometimes.

LIAM   Hard?

F. MICHAEL Yes.

LIAM   Talking to geezers like me, for instance?

F. MICHAEL No. That's sometimes the best part, talking to people. Trying to help them. *(pause)* It's the sacrifices you have to make.

LIAM   What, like no birds an' that?

F. MICHAEL Exactly. And other things.

LIAM   Like what? *(pause)* Like talking to people you wouldn't normally talk to?

F. MICHAEL You mustn't think I feel obliged to talk to you.

Liam gets up and walks behind Father Michael's chair.

LIAM   I ain't scared of you neither.

F. MICHAEL I'm pleased.

LIAM   I still reckon you're scared of me. I can see you shivering.

F. MICHAEL I'm not shivering. Really.

LIAM   Still, I might mug you. I might have a blade.
How do you know?

F. MICHAEL I don't.

Pause.

LIAM   If I killed you now, would that make you a
martyr?

F. MICHAEL I shouldn't think so.

LIAM   Why not?

F. MICHAEL Martyrdom is chosen for the holy.

LIAM   Hold up. I thought you was the holy.

F. MICHAEL I doubt it.

LIAM   All Priests are holy Joes. Don't give me that.
(pause) If you ain't holy, how can you tell people to be
holy? Eh?

F. MICHAEL That's one of the hardships I was telling you
about.

LIAM   Oh. I see. Blimey. I see. *(He walks around the
room thoughtfully.)* That's amazing. So if I had you, I might
not go to Hell or nothing?

F. MICHAEL Not necessarily.

LIAM   Bleedin' 'ell, you don't know where you stand.
Well, thanks a lot. Ta. That's alright then.

Liam starts to help himself to things in the room.

F. MICHAEL I thought you came here to talk.

LIAM   You ain't very quick are you? That was only an
excuse to get in here.

F. MICHAEL *(soothing)* You'll only get into trouble, really.

LIAM   Oh yeah? Who's gonna say anything? You?
Would you? I'll have to see about that, won't I? That's
fucking *marvellous,* that is. *(Liam hurls things about the*

room.) You bastards know fuck all do you? I come here. On me own. Standing at the back of the church. Fucking silent. Bleeding amazing. Not a sound. What can I have away, I thought? Candlesticks. But they're chained to the floor ain't they? Paintings. But they're all nailed to the wall. On me own ain't I? So I sit down at the back. Kill some time. First time I been in here for two years. Looking around. Stained glass windows. The faces are looking down at me. 'WHO ARE YOU LOOKING AT, BASTARDS?' I goes. I felt like smashing them, every last one. 'COME ON THEN!' I goes, 'DO YOUR WORST, WANKERS!' They fucking bottled out, the cowards. I knew they would because they're all posh bastards – nice boys – don't fight, do they? They're all in the Bible. They sit up there comfy and nice like those geezers on the telly. Well, they know *fuck all.* They bottled out to me! I could have taken any one of them. If only I could have got me hands on one of them. It's like that though, init? They don't move, none of them, these posh farts. They just look at you and hate you. *(pause. Liam looks at Father Michael. Silence.)* I know you. I know all you bastards. Try anything to get out of a good kicking. Then when your back's turned they nick you. *(pause)* I'm standing there. Looking round. I catch me breath. I'm feeling good. I've offered these saints out and they bottled down. I feel proud. I walk around like I own the place. I love it. The smell. Incense, candles, paintings and that. You ain't nowhere. You ain't worth fuck all. But it don't matter cos nothing's moving. It's all still. There ain't nothing outside this church, nothing. *(pause)* I ain't mad. I ain't crazy. I know that's what you're thinking. That's what everyone thinks. 'He's a loony.' They stuck me in. All you lot. Them geezers on the stained glass windows. I was inside. 'For me own health's sake,' they said. I ain't a loony though. They just don't know me.

Pause. Father Michael gets up, puts his arm around Liam, tries to comfort him.

F. MICHAEL Give me your address. I want to be your friend.
I want to help you.
LIAM   They put me away.
F. MICHAEL Who did?
LIAM   Me Mum. Me Dad. The authorities.
F. MICHAEL What did you do?
LIAM   I tried to hang meself.

Pause.

F. MICHAEL Why?
LIAM   I dunno.
F. MICHAEL You're not working?
LIAM   Nah. Can't get a job.
F. MICHAEL I'll help you, I promise. No, don't say anything.
I will help you and be your friend.
LIAM   You ain't scared of me?
F. MICHAEL No.
LIAM   You won't go to the police?
F. MICHAEL No. Trust me. Trust me.

Blackout. Music.
Lights up. Rory and Liam.

RORY   So this geezer goes – 'I ain't a prat, OK?'
I goes, 'I believe you.' Then I nutted him.
LIAM   Why?
RORY   He was Spurs, weren't he? Can't stand those
geezers. You can spot 'em a mile off. I think it's the smell.
North London stink, ain't it? Once you're over the river, say
goodbye to civilisation, mate. They should put barricades
on the south side. Stop the bacteria getting in. Us lot would
still be able to go to Chelsea and that, but we'd keep those

North London bastards out. Have passport checkpoints on Waterloo Bridge. Fucking rot sets in the other side of the river. Fuckin' Houses of Parliament, mate. Says it all. All those wankers trying to bring down the country. We should blow all the bastards up. *(pause)* Where'd you go today?

LIAM   Just hanging about. Not much.

RORY   I thought you said you was gonna be down the pub dinner-time?

LIAM   I forgot.

RORY   Mick was asking for ya. He ain't seen you for a while.

LIAM   He's a prat.

RORY   What? Don't let him hear you say that.

LIAM   You ain't scared of him are you?

RORY   Oh yeah. It was you I was thinkin' about.

LIAM   Leave it out.

RORY   What's the matter with you? You ain't half funny these days. It's that bird ain't it? She's turned you into a Zombie mate.

LIAM   Give it a rest.

RORY   She has though, son. What you doing with a bird like that? Butter wouldn't melt, eh? University birds. Can't trust 'em. You need A levels just to talk to 'em. Mind you, they all go don't they?

LIAM   She ain't like that. She's different.

RORY   How'd you mean?

LIAM   She's normal. She ain't posh or nothing. You can talk to her. About anything.

RORY   She's tasty. I'll give you that. *(pause)* She don't like me though, does she?

LIAM   What?

RORY   She bleedin' ignores me. Too bleedin' good for me, I suppose.

LIAM   She don't mind you. Not every bird's gonna throw themselves in front of you.

RORY   That's true. But I'm telling you she's changed you. You ain't no fun no more. It's affecting your football too. First time I seen you bottle out last Saturday.

LIAM   Who bottled out?

RORY   Remember that Paki geezer? You did nothing. Just stood there. If it weren't for me you'd be tucking into Hospital nosh by now.

LIAM   Oh, leave off.

RORY   I ain't getting at you. I just reckon you should be with us lot. Know what I mean, Lee?

LIAM   Yeah, I do. I know what you mean.

RORY   Nice one. I'll tell the lads you'll be down the boozer, then. Fuckin' monster good ruck tomorrow night. Friendly with Millwall. See ya.

Rory exits. Music. Blackout.
Spot on Liam, alone.

LIAM   Thigh deep mud, deep blood. Video shops. Porn houses. Women as mud. Makes you want to cough your guts, pukey and spunk. I stand here. Down the market, sauna – massage parlour. Where's the beauty? Where's the hope? Pox faced, clean shirts, posh in their comfy motors. I stand here looking at them. Sacrifice meself, that's what I'll do. I can't hold onto it. Masses of day in day out hate and chips. Vinegar battered pizzas, gristly meat pies, nothing genuine. I want some honesty. For *God's sake!* I'm perched. Settled. Balanced between the gift and the grave. The sun and the sane. It's ME mate! Fucking ME! I'm ME! I ain't a fucking person you ignore on the street. I'm ALIVE! I've GOT feelings! I NEED friends! Sure... Accent? Is that it? The way I speak...? Does that mean I don't think? Does that mean I don't FEEL, you bastards? I love you and hate you. I could fuck you and kill you. I wanna show love. I don't give a fuck what you think. I LOVE YOU! *(Screaming)* OK? OK? OK? OK? OK? LISTEN TO ME!

Blackout. Music.
Spotlight on Julia, alone.

JULIA   'Oh, he's so strong, so masterful.' What? I see that. Yeah. There's something beyond the hackneyed, something real. Terrified. Women are so much *more*. We're expected to be so much more. More understanding, more peace-keeping, more protective. Shit. The amazing thing is he doesn't expect that of me. He doesn't expect anything or demand like so many so-called liberal thinkers. Emotional fascists, most of them. Kids. I think that's why I have him around me. Possibly even love him. First thing, crisp-crumpled in the morning I can love his innocence. His remarkable silence. His tragic death wish. Is that it? I met him at a club. He was standing at the bar with his brother. I looked at him. I wanted him. I felt so horny. The shape of his head, his hair, the line of his nose, the way he stood – struck me. I went to the bar. His brother started some pathetic chat-up line. I felt sorry for him. He offered to buy me a drink. I bought my own. I saw him later on down the front near the band, so I joined him. We danced. I asked him back to my flat. He told his brother to tell their mum where he was. He was amazing. Totally insatiable. An innate sense of timing and touch. It's his genius. That's the only word for it. We have a friendship of sorts. He's at once ignorant and brilliant. I have him around. Yeah. I don't feel uneasy about it. It's clean, pure, vulgar and tasty. He feels uneasy at times. He's a lonely, isolated person. *(Beat)* Some facts, OK. My father's a doctor, my mother's a social worker. I was the Zuleika Dobson of my time at Cambridge. 'A star'. Big deal. I've got over the guilt now. I don't feel it exists anymore. Nevertheless, I'm still refreshed by his honesty. It reminds me what a bunch of idiots I've mixed with most of my life. The public school boys with their patronising please, thank you and fuck you. Their smarmy, all knowing glances across bar rooms. Their pathetic attempts at second-hand eroticism. Their utter fear of women. Their seedy innuendo and seething condescension. Their whiskings-off to country seats and delicately perfumed baronial mansions. Clean aired and functional. Or scatty, rumpled and studied bohemianism. Roughing it at Cambridge on enormous gifts from their parents. Sitting on the floor passing round joints and red wine and being 'real' with each other in assumed regional accents. And I was such a fool. I was actually impressed by this in my first year. I was so green. I grew up. I realised where I was. I stood on my own feet. I needed no one. *(Beat)* Then he steams into my life, as he would call it. I love his cheekiness, his serious wonderment. I like him. He refreshes me.

Blackout. Music.
Lights up. Father Michael's study. Father Michael and Liam.

LIAM	It ain't right.
F.MICHAEL	What?
LIAM	Me and her. It ain't right.
F.MICHAEL	Why not?
LIAM	Well, I've – I dunno.
F.MICHAEL	You've made love? Is that it?
LIAM	Yeah.

Pause.

F.MICHAEL	And?
LIAM	What do you mean... and? Ain't that enough?

F. MICHAEL   Why do you say that?

LIAM   We fuck. She fucks me. I fuck her. We fuck.

Pause.

F.MICHAEL   Do you love her?

LIAM   I dunno.

F.MICHAEL   Do you?

LIAM   Yeah. Sort of. Yeah.

F. MICHAEL   She loves you?

LIAM   Course. She says so.

F.MICHAEL   Then what's the problem?

LIAM   You should know that. It ain't the right thing to do. Sex before marriage and that. Well, I mean – I don't think it's wrong, it's just that you lot do.

F.MICHAEL   Us lot?

LIAM   Priests and that. Church.

F. MICHAEL   Listen, if you love each other and you make love together, then you're only expressing that love in a natural, honest way. *(Gently)* You won't be plunged forever into hell-fire for doing that. It's not hollow, empty or trivial. You've obviously thought about it. You're not treating it lightly. You love each other. Relax. Treat her with respect. Don't use her. What more can I say?

Pause.

LIAM   Do you know something?

F.MICHAEL   What?

LIAM   You're alright.

F.MICHAEL   Really?

LIAM   Yeah. Diamond.

F. MICHAEL Thanks. Thank you. *(pause)* Did you manage to read those books I gave you?

LIAM Hold up, I only just got them.

F.MICHAEL Take your time. I think you'll like them though.

LIAM What's all this for?

F.MICHAEL Sorry?

LIAM All this. I mean, why are you doing it? I'm only a wanker – sorry, a git. You don't owe me nothing.

F. MICHAEL You aren't a... wanker. You're not even a git. You're a friend, OK? I want you to be my friend.

LIAM Why?

F.MICHAEL I like you. I want to help you.

LIAM I don't need help.

F.MICHAEL Yes you do. You need help to open your eyes. You need help to give you strength. To make you unwind, see, feel, understand. Reach out and give. To develop your genius, your gift, your sensitivity.

LIAM *(laughing)* Bollocks!

F.MICHAEL Listen. The leader of the gang. You. And your brother. You rule London, is that what you said? You carve people up on the Fulham Road on a Saturday. You run, scream, cut, slice your way to what you think is the truth. Flow with that. But with the energy must come the love, the understanding: the compassion with the passion. You rule? What kind of strength does it take to do that? Enormous strength. Not just boots and fists, but spiritual strength. Cut away the hatred, develop the love, abandon the destruction, cultivate the creation. Don't be saddled with other people's views of you. You are intelligent. You don't need to express that by causing pain. Teach the people a lesson, yes. But find out the real enemies. Not some stranger on a street corner. Seek out the forces that would keep you in ignorance and destroy them.

LIAM *(quiet, low)* We're ten handed. Walking down the Fulham Road. Me and Rory in front. There's twenty of them

at least. They' re getting closer. I feel the energy rising.
Closer. You can see their faces, what they look like, what
they're wearing. They look heavy. Hard. Rory says nothing.
No one says nothing. It's like slow-motion. I know us lot
are secretly shitting it. Even Rory. I can sense that he's
scared, but he won't turn back. My throat feels like
sandpaper, my legs are water. They aren't turning back.
We ain't turning back. It's like a fucking Western or
something. Closer... High noon. People on the other side of
the street stop what they're doing. Shoppers come out of
shops, stand in doorways. Model birds and geezers in
porsches stare like dead sheep. No fucking life. Closer...
I ain't scared. I'm excited. People lean out of windows.
Everyone looking at us, like the Albert fucking Hall or
Madison Square Garden or something. Fucking star
attraction. Really close now. There ain't no sound. Just
blink and you're there. I'm General fucking Custer. Or
Charge of the Heavy Brigade. 'WANKER!' someone shouts.
I start running. Closer... closer... closer... BULLS EYE!
BANG ON TARGET! My boot's gone out, flattens someone's
balls. Elbow in the nose. Headbutt in face. Someone flashes
out a tool. One of our boys has a pickaxe handle. Bottles
come easily to hand. I whip one around this hard geezer's
face – their leader. 'YOU BASTARD, take that!' Some
geezer's got me brother on the deck. 'I'll have him,' I goes.
Straight in. No worries. I maimed the bastard. Pulled him
off, slammed him on the deck, jumped on his head, rolled
him over, booted him up the road, smashed his head into a
brick wall. 'Yeah', I goes, 'Yeah? That'll teach you to touch
my brother, ballshead.' They're fucking bricking it by this
time. Only their hardcore ain't leaving. Their leader, the
mouthy bastard, face flowing like the Thames, has this
blade and starts slashing around him, cutting up my mate's
face. Me brother gets his blade and slits his fucking cheeks
open. When his mates see this they start legging it all the
way back down the Fulham Road. *(pause)* There's peace
now. Quiet. I thought I saw dust and smoke settling,

floating down on the pavement. No sound. I look round – some of our mates a bit the worse for wear. But I felt proud of them. I felt so fucking proud I swear I could have cried. *(pause)* I'm gonna miss it.

Blackout. Music.
Lights up. Julia's flat. Liam and Julia together.

JULIA	Where did you get the book?
LIAM	Bought it.
JULIA	It's great, you'll like it.
LIAM	Yeah, I'm half way through it now.
JULIA	What do you reckon?
LIAM	What?
JULIA	The book.
LIAM	It's good.
JULIA	Why the sudden interest?

LIAM *(light)* How do you know it's sudden? I may have been a secret Einstein before I met you.

JULIA	Maybe.

Liam kisses Julia.

LIAM	I love you.
JULIA	I know you do. I know.

He kisses her again.

LIAM	I love you.
JULIA	Speak up. Can't hear you.

Liam kisses her – long.

LIAM   I said, 'Hello, mate, how's it going?'

Pause.

JULIA *(quiet)* I saw 'Anarchy' painted on a tree. On a tree. I was on the bus. I was tired, but happy. I was looking forward to seeing you. Do you know what you've turned me into...? Anyway, I was on the bus when I saw this big white circle. I looked closely and saw a big white A in the middle. It was daubed on this huge centuries old oak tree. By the side of the road. I was amazed. I don't know why. It looked as though it had been painted on painstakingly. This huge immovable oak tree shooting out of the surrounding concrete and tarmac, surviving it, even thriving. Daubed with 'Anarchy'. 'Anarchy' on a tree. Just like that.

Pause.

LIAM   Yeah. Got any grub?

JULIA   No I'm out. Got some coffee. Few biscuits. I think there's a bit of bread left.

LIAM *(melodramatic)* Bread? Bread? You expect a man to live on bread alone? What's going on here? I'm being starved to death by this mad woman. Help. Let me out. Guards. I give in. I'll tell you everything, just give me something to eat. Something to eat.

JULIA *(laughing)* You daft bugger.

LIAM   You know something. You're mad you are.

They kiss.

JULIA   Very possibly. Very possibly.

LIAM   Very possibly? You are. I can tell. I know all about that sort of thing.

JULIA   How?

LIAM   Well, when I'm with a mad person my nose starts wobbling.

JULIA *(smiling)* Oh, come on.

LIAM   No. Really. It wobbles. A mad person comes within twenty yards and it's jelly time. I tell you.

JULIA   You crazy sod.

LIAM   Do you know what happens when I meet a sexy girl who's also mad? Seaside rock and jelly. You fancy it?

JULIA   Doesn't sound like my cup of tea.

LIAM   An obnoxious concoction.

JULIA   What?

LIAM   An – obnoxious – concoction.

JULIA   What's that?

LIAM   That's what my auntie used to say. She took us down to Brighton when my mum left home that time. Me and my brother. We went into this café. We had fish and chips. I put salad cream on me chips. I love that. Salad cream and chips. It's like Mozart, Michelangelo and Chelsea rolled into one. Heaven. So, anyway I put this salad cream on me chips instead of tomato sauce and me auntie goes, 'What an obnoxious concoction.' I'll never forget what she said. I wouldn't have minded but she thought it was posh and clever to say it. She used to say it about everything. 'Ere auntie, can I wear me trainers on me head?' –'What an obnoxious concoction,' she'd go. Silly prat.

JULIA   Do you still see her?

LIAM   No. I think she married a body builder and moved to Peckham or something. She weren't even me real auntie anyway. Friend of me mum's.

Pause.

JULIA   Do you want to help yourself to some coffee
    and stuff?
LIAM   Nah. It's alright. I've got to be going soon.
JULIA   You're joking. Already?
LIAM   Yeah.
JULIA   Aren't you staying tonight?
LIAM   Nah. I can't. I've got to meet a mate of mine.
    Besides, I've got my reading to catch up on.
JULIA   This happened the other night as well. Who are
    you meeting?
LIAM   It's just a friend. *(Light)* My advisor.
JULIA   Oh yeah.
LIAM   Look, I'll try and get back. OK? Tonight. *(He
    kisses her.)* Look it ain't another girl or nothing.
JULIA   I wouldn't mind if it was. Just so long as we're
    honest with each other. Yeah?
LIAM   Yeah.
JULIA   Are you going to Chelsea on Saturday?
LIAM   Yeh. Bit of shopping in the King's Road.
JULIA *(laughs)* Come on. Are you?
LIAM   I suppose so. I'm not sure.
JULIA   Are you serious?
LIAM   What?
JULIA   You're thinking of not going to Chelsea?
LIAM *(almost to himself)* Yeah. I may not need it now. I used
    to. I used to need the place. I wouldn't have been no use
    for nothing if I lost it. But I reckon I don't need it no more.
    Do you know what I mean?
JULIA   Have you gone off them or something?
LIAM   No, I'll never go off the team. But then again it
    never was the team though, was it? It was the lads, the
    atmosphere, the aggro. Something to do. Being a part of
    them.

JULIA *(laughs)* I don't believe it. I thought I'd never hear you say that. Are you OK? I mean, you're not ill or anything are you? *(pause)* You'll be telling me you've found a job next. Beat me to it, I can see. *(pause)* It's something else though isn't it? You're gentler. Not as paranoid. Not as worried? You haven't turned up here covered in shit and blood for a fortnight. You're more human. More open, relaxed.

LIAM *(quoting)* Listen, I'm cutting away the hatred, developing the love, abandoning destruction and cultivating the creation.

JULIA   What? Where did you read that?

LIAM   I never read it. You are creation, right? I'm cultivating ya. Simple.

JULIA   Simple. You bastard. I love you.

She kisses him long and hard. There is a knock at the door.

JULIA   Who?

LIAM   I dunno.

Julia goes to the door, opens it. Rory stands in the doorway with a can of lager.

RORY   Evening all. This is your local candidate for the wankers' party. May I enter?

JULIA   By all means.

Rory enters.

RORY   By all means. Ain't she a lovely little wordsmith?

LIAM   What you doin' here?

RORY   I like that. That's the welcome he gives his big brother when he pops round to meet the missus. Charming ain't he?

JULIA   How are you?

RORY   OK. Bearing up under the strain of success. It's tough going though, what with the upkeep of the two mansions and my villa in the south of France. Truth to tell, success hasn't spoilt me. I'm still the fun-loving boy-next-door type you all knew and loved.

LIAM   You're pissed.

RORY   Hold up, son. What sort of language is that to use in front of a lady? Yes, old man, I'm slightly inebriated. That's better, ain't it? Inebriated. Sounds like a ferret with diarrhoea.

LIAM   How did you know where to come?

RORY   You gave the address to Mum on the back of an envelope, remember? In case of emergencies.

LIAM   But I...

RORY   You told her not to give it to no one. Meaning me. I found it in her handbag.

LIAM   I never said that.

RORY   She gets worried about you, staying out all hours with strange women. No offence.

JULIA   Do you want some coffee or something?

RORY   Well, don't sound too desperate about it, will you? No thanks. I've brought me own liquid refreshment. Transportable size. *(Drinks)* Dear me. How rude of me. Would you like a drop, darling?

JULIA   No thanks. And listen, I'm not your darling.

LIAM   She ain't my darling, Rory. She don't like that word.

RORY   Don't you? Sorry darling. Never meant no harm by it. Well. Ain't you gonna ask me to sit down?

JULIA   Yeah. Help yourself.

Rory sits.

RORY   Ta. Well, this is cosy, innit? Must say though, it's a bit threadbare, ain't it? Bit under-decorated. Don't you reckon, Liam?

LIAM   What?

RORY *(through gritted teeth)* A bit threadbare? The decor like? *(Bright)* Mind you, it ain't nothing to do with me. I'm just an ignorant cunt. Don't mind me. No offence. 'Scuse my language. *(Long pause)* Hold up a mo'. Hold up. Thinks: I get the distinct impression I ain't welcome here. I get the distinct impression I've come at a bad time. Rory, my son, I think you've done a no-no on this one. I think you're out of order my son. *(To Julia and Liam)* Sorry, just thinking aloud.

LIAM   Where you been tonight?

RORY   Here and there, son. Here and there. I was in the pub tonight. You weren't there. Again. I thought you said you would be.

LIAM   I couldn't make it tonight, though.

RORY   When are you gonna start makin' it? People are asking questions about you. It puts me in a funny position, son. I can't keep covering up for you.

LIAM   Well, don't then. You don't have to.

RORY   Hold up. This is very rude. We're taking over the conversation. This ain't polite. Sorry love. Join in. Tell us a funny story.

JULIA   No, it's OK.

RORY   Do you mind me being here? Only I can go somewhere else with my brother and have a chat in private if you like.

LIAM   I ain't got time. I've gotta meet someone.

RORY   Oh yeah? Who?

LIAM   A friend.

RORY   A friend? You're keeping yourself to yourself these days, ain't ya? I'm your brother, sunbeam. Don't say *a friend* like that to me. *A friend?* What sort of fucking talk's that?

LIAM   It's just a friend. Come on.

RORY   Who is it? What you up to?

LIAM *(shouting suddenly)* Mind your own fucking business, you nosey bastard!

RORY   I beg your pardon? Would you care to repeat that brother dear? Come on.

LIAM *(calming down)* Look, it don't matter. I never meant to get riled. Sorry mate.

The tension relaxes slightly.

RORY   That's better. Come on, let's go down the pub. You and me. We've still got plenty of time.

LIAM   I'd like to, mate, but I've got to meet someone.

RORY   Who?

LIAM   It's just a mate of mine.

RORY   Do I know him?

LIAM   Nah.

Pause.

RORY   Well, this is nice, innit? Nice cosy chat. Can't beat it. *(pause)* Doyou know what? They've opened up another chinky takeaway by the bus stop. Fucking animals they are. Chinks. You never know what you're eating, do you? It's all covered in that sickly sauce. They nick pets and cook 'em. There's only one cat left round our place and that's got three legs. Geezer dies after eating one. On my life. It was in the South London press. OK. Don't believe me, then. But when you've eaten your Chicken Chow Mein from the Fuck Ho Ho Dung and you snuff it, don't come crying to me. *(pause)* Yeah. I reckon you should do this place up a bit, give it a bit of a spring cleaning. No offence. Mind you, some people like it like this, don't they? Only yesterday in *Vogue* they had a lovely article on how to create a sparsely furnished open plan townhouse. Fucking decent, I tell you. Mind you, I thought you could have afforded a bit better, love. I thought your parents was rich?

LIAM Leave it out.

RORY Fuck me, though. If our Mum and Dad had the money we'd be living in Park Lane, son.

JULIA Come on, what is it? What do you want?

RORY Ain't she forward? I'm getting embarrassed.

JULIA Why are you so shitty tonight?

RORY I ain't shitty. I thought I was being witty. And entertaining. I am sorry. Feel short-changed? Want your honest money back? Sorry love. No refunds once the film's started.

JULIA Yeah. But I've seen this movie before.

RORY *(hard)* I'm all for re-runs, OK? Good that, eh?

Pause.

JULIA *(to Liam)* Listen, hadn't you better be going?

RORY No. He's enjoying our company. He doesn't always get the chance to talk to such intelligent, witty, entertaining people, does he? Don't want to spoil his fun. Ain't I right?

LIAM I suppose so. I was late as it was anyway. Alright if I stay here tonight?

JULIA Course it is. You sure you don't want to go?

LIAM *(sharp)* Yeah. I wouldn't have said it otherwise.

RORY That's right. You make up your own mind. That's more like it. So, we're going down the pub then?

LIAM Nah. Don't fancy it.

Uncertain pause. Liam and Julia are not sure how Rory will react.

RORY   Did you know what would happen if you balanced three thousand ants end to end without knocking them over and fed them on a diet of boiled mushrooms for three years, then a diet of elephant shit for another three while being careful only to drink lager for the duration of the said time?

LIAM   What?

RORY   Nothing.

Liam stares at Rory. Starts laughing. They laugh together.

LIAM *(laughs)* You mad bastard.

RORY   Home game Saturday. You coming?

LIAM   I dunno.

RORY   Course you are. Can't miss it again. You ain't been for three weeks.

JULIA *(hard)* He doesn't want to go. OK?

RORY   Excuse me. This ain't nothing to do with you.

JULIA   Oh yeah? It's got everything to do with me. I can see what it's doing to him. All of you lot. He's not like you. Can't you see that? He's trying to get rid of all that shit. He doesn't have to fuck, drink, tell stories and kill people to make you bastards laugh anymore. Can't you let him go?

Pause.

RORY   Well, well. There's one thing I hate. That's hearing a woman swear. Know what I mean? It just ain't right.

JULIA   Then why don't you just fuck off? I don't want you here any more. OK?

RORY   I'm afraid it ain't that easy. I'm here with my brother. OK? *(pause)* You've never liked me have you? Who do you fucking think you are? Just cos I blew you out down that Club ain't it? You've never forgiven me for that. My heart bleeds, it really does.

JULIA   I don't believe this. What are you talking about? You seriously believe that? I blew you out, friend, and don't make any mistake about it.

Liam gets up, moves away from them. Goes to the other side of the room.

RORY   Just button your lip, darling. I don't want to insult my intelligence talking to you. I'm delicate like that.

JULIA *(firm)* Now. I've told you. Shift your arse out of that door.

RORY *(to Liam)* Are you gonna let your bird talk to me like that?

LIAM *(agitated, intense)* Just leave it out the pair of you. Stop it.

JULIA   Come on. Get out. Leave us alone.

RORY   Shut your gob, OK?

LIAM *(shaking)* Stop it.

JULIA   Can't you see what you're doing to him? Just leave him alone. Can't you just let him go? Just drop it, for God's sake.

RORY   Let him go? What the fuck you on about?

JULIA *(low)* You can't see it can you? You can't see the damage. There's no joy, is there? No hope? Just pride and shit and swagger. You're loveless. You know that? Now that he's reaching out and finding love you won't allow that, will you? You with your close knit Irish London Council House pride. But it's not pride is it? You're even ashamed of it.

Is that why you submerge yourself in booze, go out on the
stands and the street carving people up? Why don't you
take pride? Pride. For fuck's sake – you've got enough
energy to keep London alight for years. It's amazing. Why
don't you use it?

RORY   What *is* she talking about?

*Liam has been startled, shaking during this exchange. He runs
into the centre of the room, screaming:*

LIAM   Oh When The Blues
                    Go Steamin' in
                    Oh When The Blues Go Steamin' In
                    I Wanna Be In That Bundle
                    Oh When The Blues Go Steamin' In

Rory joins in

                    Oh When The Blues
                    (Oh When The Blues)
                    Go Steamin' In
                    (Go Steamin' In)
                    Oh When The Blues Go Steamin' In
                    I Wanna Be In That Bundle
                    Oh When The Blues Go Steamin' In
                    Chelsea! Chelsea! Chelsea!

*Liam and Rory start jumping up and down as if they were in a
fight. All this is a strange, intense, manically fast ritual
between them.*

RORY   I get my blade out.
LIAM   Sharp.
RORY   I slash it once.

LIAM   Fast.

RORY   I push it in.

LIAM   Nice.

RORY   I pull it out.

LIAM   Great. I'm great. I'm in there. I pull the bastards balls off. I brain him.

RORY   Yeah.

LIAM   I fucking slash his throat.

RORY   Right.

LIAM   I mangle his skull.

RORY   Fast.

LIAM   I pull. I kick. I shout. I scream. I lick. I fuck. I scream. I burst.

RORY   Sharp.

LIAM   I tear, throttle, maim... Cunt Shit Bastard Arsehole Prick Wankers.

RORY   Shits.

LIAM   Posh telly cunts in the stands.

RORY   Slash'em.

LIAM   Season ticket wank piles.

RORY   Murder.

LIAM   Everyone. Everyone.

RORY   HAVE 'EM OVER!

LIAM   You're outside. You're waiting... We're mob handed, they're dead. We're alive. We're running technicolour dream kids. Electra glide in red. The pack that slice. Brainy. Clever, sharp. Run. Riot. Splurge. We're electric. Electro-magnetic. We travel. Campaigns. Away games. Glory. Death. Blood and Iron. RAGE... SCREAM... RAMPAGE... BLOOD-SPLASH... We leave nothing to chance. We are THE BOYS. The glory boys of death and celebration. We love what we do. We are passionate. We love people's hatred of us. WE ARE CHELSEA. The young mentals. The flying squad. The Heaven and Hell squad

of London village. RIGHT? YOU HEAR THAT, ARSE-HOLES?
YOU AWAKE? THIS IS ME TALKING, LONDON. OPEN UP
YOUR FUCKING EARS AND LISTEN.

*Liam collapses in a sweating heap on the floor. Silence. Rory,
who has stopped halfway through Liam's outburst, is now
staring at him. Julia is pressed up against the wall in shock
and fear.*

RORY *(to Julia)* What have you been doing to him?

JULIA   What?

RORY   Didn't he tell you?

LIAM   Don't.

RORY   He was inside for his loony behaviour. Me Mum
and Dad had to have him put away.

LIAM *(from the floor. Low, strangely articulated)* Mad? There
is inside some madmen – not me maybe – there's a kind of
genius yeh you see 'em in books yeh no one gets 'em and
their imaginations and their love burning in their heads so
madness is their only escape from the trap that's been set
for 'em.

Silence.

RORY   What the fuck you on about? Did you do this?
Did you introduce him to the art of speaking like a wanker?
You bitch. What have you done to him?

JULIA *(goes to Liam, sits next to him on the floor.)* Are you
OK, love?

RORY *(after a brief pause)* I've had just about enough of this.
Oi, brother dear. Get up. We're going.

JULIA *(with strength)* He's staying here.

RORY *(hard)* I wanna know. I wanna know why he ain't been
down Chelsea the last three games. I wanna know why

he ain't talking to his fucking mates no more. I wanna know why he's turning into a fucking ponce. I'm his brother. I got a right to know.

JULIA *(quiet, cradling Liam on the floor, as if to herself)* There weren't many of us on the bus. About seven altogether. This old woman got on. No one helped her. I just sat there, watching her struggle. I wanted to help but I was rooted to the spot. I couldn't move. It was a mixture of embarrassment and fear. I watched her. She managed. She coped. For no apparent reason I suddenly felt like crying. I felt like weeping for her and all of us. I couldn't understand exactly why. Then it dawned on me later. She had been rejected – forced to travelling on buses at her age – we failed to help her. Because she no longer produced. She was of no use anymore.

Pause.

RORY *(to Liam)* Oi, you coming now?

JULIA No. He's not coming. He's staying here. He needs help. He's balanced very precariously at the moment and you're not pushing him over. I'm telling you. You're taking him from here over my dead body. He's like me. He needs help, understanding. He wants to be strong, without the death of so much else that usually comes with what we call strength. For God's sake just leave him alone. He doesn't want to play the manly crap. He doesn't want to be confronted with cheap images of women that he can wank to. He wants the real thing. And he's got it, boy. Is that what you're jealous of? That he's becoming stronger than you when he admits he doesn't have to hurt someone just because they're wearing different colours? Or because they look at him for too long in the pub? He's told me. He doesn't need it. So leave, OK?

Pause.

RORY   So that's it? This is what you've been saying to her? She's fucking ruined you, son. I never want to see you again. Do you hear that, you wanker?

LIAM   It ain't just her, Rory. It's me. I'm in the church right. *(Getting up)* I'm all alone. It smells nice. Heavy black rain outside. I was walking in it. Down Sharp Street. Past the *Rose And Crown*. I was going nowhere. The pubs were shut. I was bored. I saw the church the other side of the street. Went in. Opened the heavy wooden door. Flowers on the altar. The little red light. Silent. I could hear the rain outside. I coughed. It sounded like God. It echoed round the building. Like it was absorbed by all the wood, all the stone. I sat down. So quiet. I could hear my own blood running through my veins. I got up and went through the pass door. I thought I might nick something. Then I saw this bloke. It was a priest. I started talking. Bit of a laugh. I was gonna do him. *(pause)* He talked to me, Rory. He talked to me like no one's ever done before. He listened an' all. It's like it's all rich and new. Know what I mean? I'm reading, Rory. I'm reading books. Imagine that. You should meet him. He's like my mate. I ain't gone all religious or nothin'. It's just something else in my life. Something new. I don't feel like a prick no more. Know what I mean?

Long pause. Rory stares at Liam. He goes to him as if to embrace him. Pause.

RORY   Wanker.

Rory goes for Liam. Kicks him in the stomach. Punches him. Bangs his head on the floor. Julia tries to stop him. He pushes her away. Rory beats Liam up. Liam offers no resistance.

RORY *(shouts)* Fight back you wanker! *(Liam does nothing. Rory leaves him semi-conscious on the floor.)* Wanker!

Don't you ever show your face down the pub no more!
You're a fucking embarrassment! You fucking tosser!

JULIA   Get out! *(She runs at Rory, grabs him by the
collar, shakes him.)* You bastard! You stupid bastard!

*Rory stares at what he's done. Lights snap to blackout.
Spotlight on Julia, holding Liam. Music.*

JULIA   Grief doesn't begin here.
It starts without these things,
It can start in the womb.
Grief doesn't need encouragement.
Ignorance coughs blood in the air.
Terror pianos of guilt.
His music,
His silence,
I've seen him fighting.
He fights nothing.
I feel depressed soul down.
I trust nothing.
I believe nothing now.

*Blackout.
Spotlight on Rory, alone.*

RORY   Take a look at me, right? What do you reckon
you're seeing? Yeah. Me. I'm here. I ain't dead. What don't
kill me makes me better. I'm strong. I'm hard. I don't fall
easily for lies. Not like him. I can see through their lies.
Oxford and Cambridge? You're poison. Arsenic that eats my
guts. Politicians? You're poison. With your ignorant, empty
smiles. Job Schemes? You're poison. Making me work for
bollocks money instead of a decent slab for me graft.
Probation officers? You're poison. You pretend you're
interested but you're all in it for the money – what you can
get. Church? You're fucking double poison. You lie,

you cheat, you turn people into well-behaved wankers. Don't nick this, don't smash that, don't swear or you'll go to Hell. Well, fuck it. I don't need that. I fucking reject that shit. I knew one priest who was alright. Father Healy. We played football together. Used to give me fags. He was a good geezer. Not like a priest, know what I mean? If you ain't thick and don't swallow all that shit, they use the other way: fill your head full of bullshit and lies and posh books, written by arseholes with rich parents and too much time on their hands. Make you think your life ain't meaningless so they can give you a false sense of security, then when it's too late you realise what they've done. They've turned you into an unthinking wanker. *(shouts)* They've cut your balls off! *(pause)* Well, they ain't doing that to me. I've made my stand. I've chosen to ignore their fucking lies and hatred. I wanna *(shouts)* go my own way! I know it ain't gonna be easy. It ain't easy having people hate you cos of the way you are or because you don't take their rules. But I'm gonna find it. A better fucking way, my way. I don't know what it is yet but I'll find it. I'm gonna stand on my own two feet. I don't enjoy hurting people, carving 'em up but that's the only fuckin' way I know. I ain't gonna be soft-soaped and I ain't gonna be lied to. They've offered me their poison. But I ain't drinking it. They've tried to castrate me. But I'll be in there. I'll get the knife first and I'll be in there ON ME OWN. That's the only way I know. Take a look at me, right? What do you reckon you're seeing?

Blackout.
Lights fade up. <u>Father Michael's study.</u> He is sitting down, reading. Music. Rory enters, exactly as Liam did, silent, staring.

RORY   Good book?

F. MICHAEL Sorry?

RORY   Good book?

F. MICHAEL Yes

RORY What is it?

F. MICHAEL Proust.

RORY What?

F. MICHAEL Marcel Proust.

RORY Who's he?

F. MICHAEL He was a writer.

RORY He ain't alive then?

F. MICHAEL No

RORY You mean he's dead?

F. MICHAEL Well, yes.

RORY I see. *(Pause. Rory stares at Father Michael.)* You're reading a book written by a dead man?

F. MICHAEL Yes. I suppose I am.

RORY Why?

F. MICHAEL Who are you? Do I know you?

RORY Why?

F. MICHAEL Well, it's a very good book.

RORY I know. I've read it.

F. MICHAEL Really?

RORY Yeah. Surprising is it?

F. MICHAEL No. It's just you didn't seem to recognise the name when I told you.

RORY Does that matter?

F. MICHAEL No.

RORY I've read it, OK? *(Rory walks over to Father Michael, takes the book, opens it.)* Yeah. As I thought.

F. MICHAEL What?

RORY Fucking shit.

F. MICHAEL Why's that? I think it's brilliant.

RORY Oh no. It ain't. It's irrelevant.

F. MICHAEL Why?

RORY   It don't mean nothing to me.

F. MICHAEL Who are you?

RORY   Who am I? I'm the bad one. The nasty one. The one who don't want your shit.

Pause.

F. MICHAEL What are you doing here?

RORY   Oh, I see. You don't want me here? I thought you lot was supposed to be all welcoming an' that.

F. MICHAEL Sit down. Do you want to talk?

RORY   Oh yeah. I want to talk alright. There are things I want to talk to you about.

F. MICHAEL Please do.

RORY   Oh fuck. Why are you lot always so *nice?* Will you stop being so *nice* please. Do you lot shit or what? I mean, are you human? I've often wondered.

F. MICHAEL What's the matter?

RORY   You are, sunbeam. It's you I've come to talk about. I don't reckon you're quite right. I reckon there's something seriously wrong with ya.

F. MICHAEL Well sit down and we'll talk about it.

RORY *(ignores this, walks around the room)* You've got a nice place here.

F. MICHAEL Thanks.

RORY   It weren't a compliment, China. It's an insult.

F. MICHAEL What?

RORY   An insult. The way you live. The way I live. They ain't the same.

F. MICHAEL I see.

RORY   Do you? Do you? I don't reckon you do. I don't reckon you understand nothing about me. The way I have to live.

F. MICHAEL Really.

RORY   Yeah. So what are you doing here? Why should you be here, telling everyone how to live? It ain't right.

F. MICHAEL I don't even know you.

RORY   Well, you should do. I'm in your Parish, right? You should have visited us. Me Mum's always complaining about how you never come round our house.

F. MICHAEL I haven't been here very long. A year.

RORY   A *fucking year?* Look what that geezer Moses did in a year.

F. MICHAEL *(laughs)* I know.

RORY   Yeah. One butcher's at the burning bush and he was away. He never wasted no time.

F. MICHAEL Yes, but Moses didn't have a Bishop breathing down his neck or fund-raising or youth clubs to organise.

RORY   This is true. But at least he did what he had to. He had bottle.

F. MICHAEL Bottle?

RORY   Guts, mate. He had guts. You ain't.

F. MICHAEL Hold on a minute. What do you want from me?

RORY   Now there's a question. I want some answers from ya.

F. MICHAEL Go ahead.

RORY   Right. I wanna know... I wanna know what you've been doing to Liam.

F. MICHAEL Liam? Are you Rory?

RORY   I might be.

F. MICHAEL I've heard a lot about you. I wanted to meet you.

RORY   I never wanted to meet you. I just want to know what you've done to Liam. You and that bird of his. You've taken his soul away. You've destroyed him. He ain't got no guts no more. Guts mate. That's what he had. I've always loved him for that. His bottle. Is that what you're all so jealous of? His guts? Cos you ain't got none, he ain't got a right to have none? Why didn't you just leave him alone?

F. MICHAEL Liam came to me for help. Friendship.

RORY   Oh, so I never gave him that? Ta.

F. MICHAEL I'm not saying that. He loves your – bottle – too. But he wants a different kind of friendship. That's why he came to me.

RORY   Different?

F. MICHAEL He wanted to show his love in a positive way. To you as well. He loves you very much. But also to his girlfriend. He loves her in a different way.

RORY   What about you? Does he love you?

F. MICHAEL I hope so. Yes, I think he does.

RORY   Yeah, his love is different. It's an hard love. Our kind of love. Just stick with your own cos that's the only way we can win.

F. MICHAEL Win?

RORY   It's a battle, mate. A battle for your dignity. For your self-respect. If you lose that you ain't got nothing. *(pause)* Look, all I know is, he used to be my mate. Now I ain't got him. I've lost him. He might as well be dead. He might be my brother but he might as well be a total stranger now. Thanks to you.

F. MICHAEL Rory, be patient with him. He's changing, yes. But he'll be able to love you in a fuller, more positive way. Bear with him. He's just finding his way.

RORY   But it ain't his way, is it? It's your way and her way. Not his. Just leave him alone, OK? Don't touch him no more. You've done enough damage.

F. MICHAEL No. I must help him. I've got to be able to help him.

RORY *(increasingly angry)* Ain't you done enough? Just leave us alone will you? Leave us alone! We don't need your help! He's dead now! Dead! Not alive! He's dead like the writers you read and the chat you give! You've ruined him!

Teachers, prisons, job centres couldn't beat him but you
have! Well I hope you feel proud! I hope you're satisfied!

*Rory attacks Father Michael. He beats him up, leaves him for
dead. He exits.*
*Lights change. Liam enters. Tries to revive father Michael. He
can't. Lights change.*
*Father Michael and Liam in separate spots. Music. (Boy
Soprano: Pie Jesu, Fauré Requiem).*

F. MICHAEL I speak to you now of love.
I too feel the need for extravagant aggressive genius.
Speak to me of freedom and I will show you
the landscape of truth.
I will take you there.
Sanctus Dominus. Bless me in death.
Et Resurexit...
It matters. Gloria.
I speak to you now of love.
I too feel the way forward through the black.
I trust you to know this beyond me,
Beyond time.
It might not make sense...
Perhaps that is the world's numb emotion,
Crouched in the womb with a handgun.
I fail to feel the drenching hate of ignorance
I trust to blind myself on the road to light.
Have faith.
The anonymous voice on the intercom.
I have been there.

Fade to black.
Lights snap up. Liam stands in a spotlight with a petrol bomb.
*Lights fuse. Liam runs forward to throw it towards the
audience. Stops. Extinguishes fuse. Music continues. (Pie Jesu,
Fauré Requiem)*

LIAM   Beauty, hope.
                  Here but dead.
                  Show love here and you're dead.
                  I choose the gift.
                  I choose the sun.
                  The sane can wait.

*He takes off his shirt and pours the contents of the petrol
bomb over his head. He strikes a match and is about to light
the petrol.*

LIAM   We will win.
                  We will win.

*Hold the light on Liam for a few seconds.
Blackout.*

The end.

This Other Eden

First performed by Soho Theatre Company, London in 1990.
Directed by Michael Kingsbury.

CHARACTERS	CAST
Hannah	**Maggie Shevlin**
Dave	**Dorian Healy**
Sue	**Helen Patrick**
Ken	**Shaun Curry**
Da	" "
Patrick	" "

ACT ONE
SCENE 1

Music loud. Big bass riffs pounding. Blackout.
In the darkness the music gets louder, deafening.
In the darkness on a radio feedback – the odd disjointed
optimistic passages of the social and architectural manifesto
for Airport Estate. This is done with the bass in rhythm.
Spotlight finds a disembodied hand attached to a spray can.
Spraying on to a wall 'All bastards round 'ere Round 'ere all
bastards'. Blackout.
Silence. Lights up.

HANNAH   See this is where I live. Airport Estate. Tall and
lovely. Lovelily dreadful. Built on the old London Airport,
Croydon. The East End, moved to the work-plenty suburb.
A concrete desert surrounded by an oasis of comfortable
snobbery. The Old Days. Jim Mollison and Amy Johnson,
crowds of flag-waving flesh. The earth-bound seeing off the
high flyers. Zooming, sailing off into space up there in their
bits of balsa-wood and string flying machines. Flying off

into the sky of fame and fortune. You can still see part of the runway round the back of our Close. I used to close me eyes and think of the planes taking off. The tarmac of the Second World War. Now it's over-grown. The only flying here now is when the rich kids from outside come with their dads to play with their remote-control models. Remote control.

Blackout.

DAVE   Bleeding insult. Thing about this place is – you've got to know the short cuts. People are after ya all the time around here.

VOICE   Oi! Dave! Kev told his brother you were after him with hammer.

DAVE   It weren't true. He told his big brother that so they're after me and my mates. So you've gotta know the short cuts. Coming back from town you can get the 157 and stop the other side of the wasteground and cut through to the back of Helena Close. Or if you come up Mollison Drive – you cut through Instone Close under the garages, left up the steps, under the shops and run for it when you hit daylight. If you come up from the other end of Mollison you cut through the park, round Moor Close past the school and into Helena that way.

Repeat: rap/sample music of the Estate Manifesto. Blackout. The Flat: Hannah, Dave and Sue kneeling saying Rosary. Ken reads paper.

HANNAH   Hail Mary, full of grace, the Lord is with you, blessed are thou among women and blessed is the fruit of thy womb, Jesus.

DAVE/SUE   Holy Mary, Mother of God, pray for us sinners now, and at the hour of our death.

ALL　　　　Amen.

HANNAH　　　Glory be to the Father, and to the Son, and to
the Holy Spirit.

DAVE/SUE　　As it was in the beginning, is now and ever
shall be, world without end.

ALL　　　　Amen.

Blackout.
The Flat: Lights up.

HANNAH *(on phone, chatty, bright)* Brigid? Yeah. Han here.
How's things? Yeah. Still the same here, yeah? Ken's still
looking for a job. And Dave. Sue's still at the chemist's.
Doing well there, yeah. My school dinners are still the best
in the Western World. Yeah. How's things over there? The
whole family? All the neighbours? Did Rory get drunk
again? Yeah. Michael came down from Dublin? Great. Long
way to Kerry. How is it? Did they ask after me? God I miss
it, Bridie. No. No I'm fine. I'm fine here. Like to move out of
this place, though. Yeah. Like to. Move the family to a nicer
flat, a better estate, yeah. Da's grave? Anything wrong?
Flowers every week, you're great, Bridie. I will. I'll visit.
It's getting the time, love. Yeah. I promise. No. Never see
the neighbours here. Never speak, no. Father said he might
do a House-Mass here. That's if Ken agrees. Yeah. Does the
house look any different? Danny cut the tree down? Why?
I thought Da wanted it left as it was. The storm? Oh yeah.
Rainy. Sunny. That air. Never see the sun here, really. No.
Fine, love. *(brisk)* Look, this'll cost a fortune, Bridie, I'd
better go. Yeah. I will. Send my love to the family will you?
I miss you all, darling. Love you. Bye. *(puts the phone
down, shrugs, sighs, smiles.)* Oh well.

Blackout.
Lights up.

DAVE　　　　I think I should go to Croydon. Yeah. That's it.
I'll get geared up. Go to *Sinatra's*. That's where they all go.
The real women. Buy a couple of drinks. I'll walk in. Stroll
up to the bar. Grin my cool mean grin at the bar-lady, cool
as a cucumber and away. Pubs ain't what it's about. I want
some real women. Women who'll appreciate my wit and
charm. I don't need a motor. I'll go back to their place.
Won't tell 'em I come from the Estate. Say I'm just in the
area from abroad. That's it. I'm over here on a special
assignment from Switzerland. That's it. I'm a banker. I've
got a private jet parked on the old Croydon Airport and I
want a few laughs. Mine'll be called – Samantha, that's it.
I'll write a poem for her on the back of a beer mat and
she'll be putty in my hands. *(pause)* Oh sod it. I'm going
down the pub.

Blackout.
<u>*Tableaux*</u>*: Very quick flashes. (5 seconds)*
*1. Flat with Ken sitting reading paper. Hannah standing with
plates. Sue and Dave at table. Blackout.*
*2. Flat with Ken sleeping with his feet up. Hannah staring at
　him. Blackout.*
*3. Flat again with Ken glued to paper. Hannah standing with
plates. Sue and Dave at table. Blackout.*

SUE　　　　Sue. Not much of a name. Sounds like a half
hushed-up fart. Don't it, though? Susan. Sloth swimming.
Thassit. *(pause. To customer)* Certainly madam. That eye-
shadow's nice on ya. Goes with your eyes. *(To herself)*
Vomit Green. *(To customer)* Yeah. No, it's very popular,
that one. *(To herself)* Is this it? Really? This what it's all
about? Now. Manageress. Yeah. I could handle that.
Charge of the beauty and cosmetics department. Women
like it. Like to make up. Change. Please themselves? Or
their crud-bag blokes? Who knows?... Yeah. Manageress.
Manage. Sort it out. Nice little flat. One of them smart

sporty cars. Independence. Gotta get there first. Gotta pay the price. Gotta say things like this. *(To customer again, bright)* Yes Madam, the smoky crushed koala chocolate velvet uses only natural ingredients.

Blackout.
Lights up on <u>*The Flat:*</u>

DAVE   So I laid him out, Sue.

SUE   Why?

DAVE   Mouthing off about ya. Heard him.

SUE   What?

DAVE   Don't like to say.

SUE   *What?*

DAVE   Called you a slag.

SUE   Well, that's nice coming from a male whore. He's got as much sex appeal as a fart in a bath.

DAVE   Yeah. What about me?

SUE   What?

DAVE   Fart in a bath or movie star?

SUE   Neither. More like a pissed version of the Hunch-back of Notre Dame.

DAVE   He's alright. We were gonna call our band after him.

SUE   What?

DAVE   'The Hunchback of Notre Dame and his Supple Bollocks.'

SUE   Yeah. Go down well on *Top of the Pops.*

DAVE   Reckon?

SUE   Yeah. Get a lot of airplay. I can just see it.

DAVE   No, maybe not. I'm glad we changed it to something more sensible.

SUE   What?

DAVE   My multi-coloured baboon shaped gonads.

SUE   Very commercial.

DAVE *(pause)* You going out tonight?

SUE   Yeah.

DAVE   Croydon Hilton?

SUE   Maybe. No I was thinking of flying to Bermuda
   for the weekend.

DAVE   There's no such thing.

SUE   What? Bermuda or the weekend?

DAVE   Croydon Hilton. It's a fig-leaf of my imagination.
   (pause) I reckon I'll pop round Buckingham Palace tonight.

SUE   She ain't in.

DAVE   How d'you know?

SUE   She's promised to take me out tonight.

DAVE   Oh yeah, I forgot.

*Hannah enters. Starts to unpack shopping. Bustling. Bright.
Busy.*

HANNAH   Hello loves.

DAVE   Hello Mum.

SUE   Alright Mum? Been to Mass?

HANNAH   Yeah. Just been to the six o'clock. Coffee club
   afterwards. Oh, the excitement. Could've done with
   something stronger. I left your tea over the pot. Did you
   get it?

SUE   Oh, was that the tea? I thought you were
   boiling the skidmarks off Dad's knickers.

DAVE   Sue.

SUE   Sorry Mum. Yeah, it was nice.

HANNAH *(laughs)* Skidmarks? I gave up trying to boil *them*
   off. The only way to get rid of them is with a laser beam

and I don't think his dole would stretch to that. *(They laugh)*

DAVE   Do they do laser beams on the National Health?

HANNAH   Listen Dave, Father Pearce was wondering why you weren't at Mass again.

Sue sniggers to herself.

DAVE   Mum, I've told ya. I'm busy.

HANNAH   Busy with what?

DAVE   This and that.

HANNAH   Well, you've got plenty of time for getting into trouble, that's for sure.

DAVE   Well, why don't you ask her to go?

SUE   Mum's given up on me. *(laughing. Irish accent)* She knows. I'm a lost soul.

HANNAH   Sue's made up her own mind, if she wants to be lapsed that's her own affair.

DAVE   That ain't the only affair, either. *(Sue and Hannah stare at him)* Look, I'll go next Sunday, OK?

HANNAH   Alright, love. *(She kisses him on cheek)*

Blackout.
The Flat: After breakfast. Hannah running around clearing breakfast things. Ken reading paper. Long period of just this. Silence. Then Hannah tries to kiss Ken, he lazily pushes her away.

KEN   I think I'll retire. I do. Man of my age. Think I will. How about Tunisia? Yeah. Could do. Spain's nice. Spanish ain't, though. Italy? I fucking hate Italy. Never been there but I fuckin' hate it. *(Hannah stares at him – language.)* Knew this geezer who went to Nairobi. Did. He just got up one morning. Looked at his missus, looked at his kids. 'I've had enough,' he thought. So he went to Nairobi. Painting the insides of brothels lime green. True story. Wonder if he got shot by guerrillas? Mind you, maybe he thought being shot by guerrillas was better than spending the rest of his life bored out of his box. Guts, though. You need guts to do a thing like that. Must be going, though, love. *(He pecks her on the cheek. Leaves. Hannah sits down, staring.)*

Blackout.
Light up.

HANNAH *(praying)* God above, dear God. Help me. Out of this little hole try and hear me. I can't talk to him so I'll talk to you. I've never asked you for big things before. Just help me. Now. I'm, well, I'm a bit - lost. Only now. I can't quite see what you want from me. Or even if you're still with me. I'm just a bit - lonely, that's all. I'm lost. Just give me some guidance, just a bit. See me. Down here. A little bit trapped. That's all. So try and help me out, darling. Thanks. *(crosses herself.)*

Blackout.
Lights up.

DAVE *(screaming)* Try it bastards, just fuckin' try it!

Blackout.
Lights up. The flat: After breakfast. Hannah clearing things away. The ritual. Ken reading the paper. Silence. Hannah tries to snuggle up to Ken. He absently moves slightly away.

KEN   That Michael Caine looks old now nowadays. He used to be a good-looking geezer. What marriage will do to a man, eh? What won't it do? Look at the state of that.

Hair ponced up like a bleedin' garden hedge. Pop stars. What a bunch of prats, eh? What Mass you going to tonight?

HANNAH   Eight o'clock. I'll leave your dinner over the pot.

KEN   Right, see you later then.

HANNAH   Yeah.

Ken goes. Hannah – an inaudible sigh. Staring blankly.

HANNAH *(praying)* So what happened? I'm sorry. It's just that I've asked you now so many times. Are you there? Where are you? What? Did you say some-thing? *(pause)* Just make it clearer. That's all I want. A bit of a clearer view.

Lights fade.
Spotlight: Dave in slow motion street fight. Hard. Raw. Passionate. Music loud. Screams at the end:

DAVE   Airport boys run from no one. I hate you posh town bastards. I'll rip you apart. Rip out yer heart.

Blackout.
Lights up on Hannah in bed with Ken. No bed necessary, could be suggested just by lighting. Actors on floor. Hannah tries to touch and move closer to Ken. He sleepily turns over. Light closes in just on desperation on Hannah's face. Sound of melancholic Irish lament or air. Da appears. The actor playing Ken moves round to stand over Hannah, his face lit by a dim, smoky light. He shouldn't be played at all 'spooky' but just natural, conversational.

DA   Han. Han.

HANNAH   God-in-Heaven-who's-that?

DA   Don't you recognise me, darlin?

HANNAH   No. It's *not.*

DA   Yes.

HANNAH   Da?

DA   That's right, darlin. Been a long time.

HANNAH   Ken!

DA   No – don't wake him up. Be quiet. He wouldn't understand.

HANNAH *(whispers)* God! Are you a ghost or something?

DA   Kind of. But it depends on what you mean by ghost.

HANNAH   This is no time for Celtic philosophy. Da, what's going on? Are you really here?

DA   Yes. In a way. Frightened, darlin?

HANNAH   Terrified.

DA   Don't be love.

HANNAH   What're you here for?

DA   Just a little chat. I felt you calling for me.

HANNAH   How? Did I?

DA   You did. I felt you. Across the bloody black hours. You know, the tired inside-out hours of eternity. A bit like one of Father Joe's sermons.

HANNAH   I'm going mad.

DA   No. God, can't you take a little vision now and again? Han you've become so English.

HANNAH   Da?

DA   Yeah?

HANNAH   Love me?

DA   Yeah. Always did. The best. Spiritual, that's what you always were.

HANNAH   Was. Maybe.

DA   You're not happy are you, sweetheart?

HANNAH   No.

DA   What?

HANNAH *(weeps a bit)* No, Da. No, I'm not.

DA *(holds her gently)* There. There.
   (Hannah feels a bit more comfortable. Looks at Da.)

HANNAH   Da? Do you remember that time when you and
   Pat were being chased by those soldiers with guns?

DA   Yeah. Oh yeah. Under the bridge you mean?

HANNAH   Yeah.

DA   Yes. They chased me and your sister down a
   boreen. I held Pat in me arms up to me chest in water as
   those black-guards took pot shots at my cattle. I'd done
   nothing. They shot them all. We were only out for a Sunday
   stroll. They were drunk and wanted a laugh. A good laugh.

HANNAH   Or the time when me, Declan and Liam came
   back from London to visit and the boys flew the Union Jack
   from the roof.

DA *(laughs)* Coves.

HANNAH   They only did it to annoy you. Skitting you.

DA   Yeah. Great lads.

HANNAHNot what you said at the time!

DA   I know.

HANNAH   And the music evenings. God, d'you remember?

DA   I do.

HANNAH   And the pipes, and the uncles and the cousins
   and you playing the fiddle.

DA   And the drinks boiling in our hearts.

HANNAH   And the singing.

DA / HANNAH *(singing quietly)*
           Some say the devil is dead,
           The devil is dead,
           The devil is dead.
           Some say the devil is dead,
           And buried in Killarney.

More say he rose again,

Rose again,

Rose again,

Rose again,

More say he rose again,

And joined the British Army.

(They laugh together.)

HANNAH   Shhh! We'll wake the old man.

DA   Can't be doing singing songs like that in England, love.

HANNAH   No. And you a leading Republican. You with your talking and organising. God, you were so handsome. A hero. You – shone for me. Lit things up.

DA   It'll go straight to me head, Han.

HANNAH *(pause)* Da?

DA   What love?

HANNAH   You weren't happy me coming over here, were you? Marrying an Englishman.

DA   I gave you my blessing.

HANNAH   But you weren't happy.

DA   Well...

HANNAH   I should never have gone to England. Should I, Da?

DA *(smiles)* Why don't you go back?

HANNAHI've been thinking about that. I'd like to, you know. On me own, maybe.

DA   How? Leave the family?

HANNAH   They'd never come with me. Ken wouldn't come.

DA   Well that's it, then, love. An Irish mother never leaves her family.

HANNAH   But Da I'm so lonely here. I don't fit in. I feel lost and scared, Da. I feel like I'm in a prison. Shut up here.

DA   You may have to just offer it up to the Lord, darlin'.

HANNAH *(smiles)* That sounds so old-fashioned, Da.

DA   Old-fashioned? What else do you expect of a spectre of my years? *(She laughs)* What about the faith? Do they keep it up?

HANNAH   Yes. Sort of. Ken never goes. I try to encourage Dave and Sue. It's hard, though, Da. I find it hard meself.

DA *(gentle)* Yeah, love. It is hard. I know. I know. But we fought for it. Got spat on and shot and despised for it. Badge of our lives. Symbol of our hope, our joy, our land. Land squeezed out of the blood of the young gods that screamed and cried and died for it. It really means something darlin'. It really means something. We must believe. We must allow ourselves to believe.

HANNAH   I know, Da.

DA   Look, I'm going to have to be going.

HANNAH   Da? Is there anything else you wanted to say to me?

DA   Yes. Don't worry, love. You'll fight through. You're from a family of warriors and chieftains and poets. The concrete little hell you're in, is here to test you. Your heart's not concrete Han. That's why it hurts. But don't let it beat you. Fight, Han. Fight.

HANNAH   Da? Is that it?

DA   No. Go back to Ireland, Han. Take the family with you. *(starts to leave)*

HANNAH   But Da! How can I? They -

DA *(leaving)* I have to go.

HANNAH   Will I see you again?

DA   Perhaps my darlin' girl. My angel. My precious. I love you.

HANNAH   I love you too Da.

Da disappears into the smoky dark. We are left with a
bewildered, worried and inspired Hannah. Blackout.
Lights up on Dave, leaning against a wall, smoking a fag.

DAVE   So I'm sitting on the top of the 233. Favourite
seat. Top deck. First seat at the front on the right. Just
above the driver's periscope window. Due to some local
poet, the warning words 'Do not obstruct driver's periscope
glass' transformed by magic into 'Do not obstruct the
driver's penis or ass'. *(Dry)* Brilliant. How many exams did
he pass, I thought. I've got me feet up on the front
window, right. There's this bloke sitting opposite. Looking
over. Had a briefcase. Heard him mutter something to
himself like 'Typical Estate Hooligan', or some-thing. See
the bus passes through the posh parts near the estate.
Then he calls me a pig. Under his breath. 'Dirty Estate Pig.'
'Ignore him', I thought. Posh tosser that he is. But he's
looking over. You know when someone's looking at you?
Then it happened. He leans over. 'Oh no', I thought, 'He's
gonna speak' then as he leans over, there was a pause
that seemed to last three million and nine years. 'Surely he
wouldn't be so stupid, I thought'. Then it comes. 'Do you
mind?' 'Do I mind?' Do I fuckin' mind? Sounds weird, but
me Mum's face. Me Mum's face, just then. I saw it. *(pause)*
I MIND LOTS YOU POSH FUCKER. I span me boots round
into his mush. Ripped him off his seat, booted his arse
down the bus. 'Yeah, I do mind'. The driver had been
seeing through his penis or glass or whatever and stopped
the bus. I just flipped the handle on the emergency doors
and legged it. Do I mind? Do I mind? What a fuckin' insult.

Lights fade.
Lights up. The flat: Morning.

SUE   Did you go then?
DAVE   Where?

SUE   Did you go to Mass, then?

DAVE   Nah. Couldn't be bothered. Went round Terry's. Played *Monopoly.*

SUE   Oh, yeah. Who won?

DAVE   No one. We got bored in the end. He cheats anyway. Keeps putting extra houses on Park Lane. All I had was an hotel in the Old Kent Road.

SUE   What's wrong with that?

DAVE   You *been* down the Old Kent Road, lately?

SUE   Right.

DAVE   The punters never pay their hotel bills, anyway.

SUE   I think you should move out the hotel business.

DAVE   Yeah. Unless I can open the *Croydon Hilton.* Stars, photographers, the works.

SUE   What you doing up so early?

DAVE   Gotta sign on today.

SUE   Oh. Where's Mum?

DAVE   Still in bed, I think.

SUE   Is she alright?

DAVE   Think so.

Ken enters, bleary-eyed.

KEN *(to Sue)* Mornin' love. *(To Dave)* Morning wanker, crud, tosspot, toe-rag, urchin, lout, whelp.

DAVE   Don't be shy, Dad, just say what's on your mind.

KEN *(to Dave)* What you doin' up so early?

DAVE *(laughs)* Great. I show me face before twelve for once and this is the welcome I get. I gotta sign on Dad.

KEN   Yeah, well it makes a change.

DAVE   What about you, then? Got some serious work on today? Got some serious drinking to do?

KEN   Watch it, you. Creative drinking, that's what it is.

SUE   Do *what?*

KEN   Gives me ideas. Helps me to think things out.

DAVE   Oh yeah. Planning your world tour? Still thinking of going to China?

KEN   Oh, less of the cheek, son. You're not too old for a good hiding. *(Dave ignores this.)*

SUE   Where's Mum, Dad?

KEN   Still in bed.

SUE   Is she OK?

KEN   I think so.

SUE   She'll be late for work. *(gives her a shout)* Mum!

KEN   Probably just tired.

Lights change to Hannah in her bed.

HANNAH   Da? Da? Please come back. Look at me still in bed, will you? I can't breathe. How can I fight when I can't even breathe? Breathe the green sea – so much love to give. So few to take it. The living green in the concrete dead grey. *(quiet, intense, passionate)* Save me Da. *Save me*. Soul Desert. Forty days and nights. Save me.

Light on Hannah snaps off. Lights back on the group.

KEN   You going to sign on looking like that? You got no self-respect?

DAVE   Look, it ain't a fashion show, Dad.

KEN   Yeah, well it ain't a Worzel Gummidge lookalike contest, neither.

SUE   Leave it out, you two.

KEN   Look at him though. Don't you mind as a tax-payer giving your hard-earned money to a specimen like that?

DAVE   Yeah, Dad. If you're gonna scrounge, you might as well be a smart scrounger. You used to only dress up on Sundays. Now you don't go to Mass, you wear your church-suit to the dole.

KEN   Scrounge, eh? Skilled mate, that's what I am. You're the only scrounger round 'ere so button it, OK?

DAVE   Alright, alright.

Hannah enters, in her dressing gown. She looks tired. Surprised reaction from the others.

KEN   You alright, love?

HANNAH   Yeah, I'm fine.

DAVE   Mum, about Mass on Sunday -

HANNAH   I know, you didn't go.

DAVE   Yeah, sorry.

HANNAH   That's OK. Doesn't matter.

KEN   Chance of any breakfast, love?

HANNAH *(distant)* I don't know. Yes I think so.

KEN   Only I'm off out in a minute and Sue's waiting to get to work.

SUE   If you ain't feeling well, Mum, I can do it.

HANNAH No, no, I'll do it. It's OK. *(gets up, walks a few steps, stops and just stands there. Pause.)*

DAVE   You alright, Mum?

HANNAH   Yeah, yes. Fine. Just – well.

SUE   Come on Mum, let me do it eh?

HANNAH *(quietly)* Mum. That's not my name, is it? My name used to be Hannah. People used to say, 'What a lovely name.' Nobody calls me that, anymore.

Sudden snap lighting change. Hannah's view.

KEN *(as a British soldier)* Army life? See the world? I been
  stuck on this shitty green island with these thickos for so
  long now I wish I'd never joined. Leather boots and cold
  steel. Anglo-Saxon way. Lovely.

*Lights snap back to normal. All look on as Hannah reacts to
this.*

HANNAH   No. Get out.
SUE   Mum?

*Hannah is confused. She looks at Sue. Sue changes to become
Hannah's idealised view of her. Lights change.*

SUE   A beautiful young Celtic princess. Maeve. A
  leader of the tribe. A fount of inspiration and victory. Life,
  young and rich and full of promise.

Lights back to normal. Everyone as they were.

HANNAH   Yes, Maeve. Yes. That's it. *(sees them all
  staring at her. She is embarrassed and confused.)*
KEN   Come on love, sit down. Have a cup of tea. *(He
  sits her down)* Ain't you gonna be late for work?
HANNAH   Yes.
KEN   If you ain't feeling well, you should take the day
  off.
HANNAH   Alright, I think I will then.
SUE   Look, shall I do some breakfast, then?
KEN   No, I'll pass on that one. You'll be late anyway,
  Sue.
SUE   OK. I'll be off then. You coming?

KEN Yeah. *(To Hannah)* I'll see ya later then, love.

SUE See ya Mum. Take care now.

They leave. Pause.

DAVE You OK?

HANNAH Yeah.

DAVE Shall I take you to the doctor's?

HANNAH No. I don't need a doctor.

DAVE Just a bit tired, eh?

HANNAH Yeah. Tired of it all. *(pause)* It's nice to be alone together, isn't it? We never seem to have time.

DAVE Yeah.

HANNAH You know something? You're different from him.

DAVE Dad? How d'ya mean?

HANNAH You've always been more like me. Even since you were a little kid. Your face glowing in the candles on a birthday cake – your eyes really huge – enquiring. You're just – different people, that's all.

DAVE Are you alright, Mum?

HANNAH No. Look, will you stop for just one second? One moment let your guard down. You know what I'm saying. Don't you think it's sad? What you once had. Completely gone now? Like me. I'm the same. Do you think this is really *me*? A school dinner lady? That Headmaster. I remember the first week I went in there. I used to know him before I worked there, from the Church. He was friendly, so I thought I'd keep up the friendship. He'd come and inspect the kitchens and I'd stop what I was doing and go straight up to him. 'Hello love, how are ya?' He'd talk, but there was always a feeling of: 'Yes, that's fine, but remember your place'. And the looks I'd get from the English women. Really annoyed. Really angry that I was so full of myself. I never stopped, though. It was like a battle every day. Assert meself. Be meself. *(pause)*.

DAVE *(quiet, remembering)* You always used to give me seconds.

HANNAH *(smiles)* And thirds sometimes.

DAVE   Yeah.

HANNAH   But is that what I really am? And you? Do you think you're just a tearaway – a hard case? 'Cos you're not love – oh it doesn't matter.

DAVE *(quiet)* What do you mean, Mum?

HANNAH   I don't know. I really don't. It's just a feeling. Like a recurring dream. It's like a room stuffed, crammed with flowers. Big, beautiful colours and smells – and I'm in the middle. There's a smile on my face. But then I see that the smile is contorted – I'm there, I'm in a funeral parlour stretched out and the room's a coffin. But there I am, still smiling. *(pause)*

DAVE *(worried)* Look, Mum do you want me to stay with you today?

HANNAH   But do you know what I'm saying? Do you understand? *(stares at him)*

DAVE *(quiet)* What's the matter? Eh? Is it 'cos I ain't going to Mass so often these days?

HANNAH   God, I don't mind. You've got to make your own mind up on that one. You know I don't even know if you're not right.

DAVE   How do you mean, Mum?

HANNAH   I stopped the new priest the other day. Outside the church. Wanted to talk to him. He seemed a nice person. We were getting on. Then I mentioned where I lived. 'Oh, the Estate', he said. He changed. He moved ever-so-slightly away from me. Shuffled from one foot to the next. Dave, he looked down on me, OK. I wasn't imagining it.

DAVE   Now you're learning. I'm used to that, Mum.

HANNAH   Yeah, but he's supposed to be God's representative.

DAVE   God's a snob, Mum. *(pause)* Sorry.

HANNAH *(quiet)* God's a snob.

DAVE   No, I was only joking.

HANNAH   No, don't back down, Dave. Don't try and spare the old girl from the fact that she's been slaving away the best years of her life for a snob. A cheat. It really means something, though. I must allow meself to believe. *(Pause. She gets up. Puts record on. Irish traditional music, featuring violin. She moves to it.)* Flying. Living on the old London Airport. This is where Chamberlain waved Hitler's bit of paper. Betrayal. Yeah. Travel. Funny. When Jim Mollison and the rest of 'em took off from here I wonder if they even thought what would come in its place. They'd have champagne and picnic hampers and taffeta. Broderie anglaise and feathered hats. Clinking of cut crystal and voices raised gently from the private enclosure. The change. Broken glass, slashed wrists and graffiti. *(pause)* Yeah. I wonder when the last person flew from here.

DAVE   Fifty years?

HANNAH   Long time ago. This place, though. Dumped in the middle of nowhere. Cut off from everything. It's done something to you. What a waste. Out of my womb, for God's sake.

DAVE   Bloody 'ell Mum, leave it out. I'm just worried about you.

HANNAH   Sometimes I look at you and wonder where you came from. Sorry, love, it's just so frustrating. All my efforts, everything I did to help you grow – wasted. What am I, against this place?

DAVE   Come on Mum.

HANNAH   I just don't want you to be apart from the rest of the world all your life. You're still young – just make a break.

DAVE   It ain't that easy, Mum.

HANNAH   Yes, it is. Sorry, love, I don't want to sound so desperate, different from how I was. It must be difficult for you. But what's all this 'big man' stuff? Eh? When you're with me you can hug me and tell me you love me without being ashamed. Why is it you're different when your mates come round? Or even with your father around?

DAVE   It's different, though, ain't it?

HANNAH   How?

DAVE   You're me Mum. I can be like that with you. But when I'm out there it's gotta be different, know what I mean?

HANNAH   No. I don't.

DAVE   I'm gonna fight, Mum. No-one'll stop me doing that. It's self-respect. It's important, OK?

HANNAH   Come on. Do you enjoy it?

DAVE   What?

HANNAH   Do you enjoy seeing people suffer?

DAVE   What's all this about? *(annoyed)*

HANNAH   Do men enjoy seeing people suffer?

DAVE   I ain't 'men,' Mum. I'm me.

HANNAH   Dave, don't ignore it.

DAVE   That's enough, right.

HANNAH   Violence. All this aggression. I could never understand that part of you Dave.

DAVE *(hard)* Look, leave it out.

HANNAH   You wouldn't hit me – not like him?

DAVE   Part of it's your fault, OK? *(pause)*

HANNAH   What do you mean?

DAVE   Violin lessons, Mum? Round 'ere?

HANNAH   What about 'em?

During this speech a fiddle takes up a slow lament.

DAVE   I'm walking down the deck between the blocks, right? I'm thirteen. Carrying me violin. I've got the latest gear on, cool trousers, good barnet, tasty shirt and a fancy walk – carrying a violin. I see Tracy on me right. I used to fancy her, OK? She's into raves and sound systems. As I get closer, she sees the violin. I keep walking. Make out I haven't seen her. Then I hear her laughing. My steps got longer. Felt like I was walking through treacle. Laughing in me ears. Then I dodged down the steps for the garages. I thought – 'That's it' – I'll take the route that goes underground beneath the garages. No one saw me. Then I made it to the edge of the estate and the bus stop for town. Then I saw 'em. Frank O'Dowd, Steve Healy and the rest of 'em. I kept me eyes straight ahead. Sat on the wall waiting for the 157. 'Oi, wanker,' I heard O'Dowd shout. Heard 'em laughing. 'Oi. Pansy-bollocks, where's yer handbag' and 'Play us a tune.' I just kept me eyes in front, praying for the bus to come. Then someone punched me in the side of the head, another punch in the guts, a clump in the gob. I grabbed hold of me violin. Wouldn't let go. They were trying to get it off me, but me knuckles were white with the holding-on. Then they had me over on the floor. Grabbed the violin. Opened the case. Forced me to play.
I was still learning, so I weren't no good. I could have been though, the teacher said. So they ripped the violin off me. Smashed it against the bus stop. I stood there. Nothing I could do. It made little noises as it was being busted up – like it's very last tune sort of thing. And I cried. I cried. Like a little fuckin' baby I cried.
(pause)
So that was it. I knew that was it. No one, nowhere was ever going to do that to me again, OK? *(beat)*
Told you I left it on the bus, remember.

HANNAH *(quietly)* I had a feeling it must have been something like that, love.

DAVE   I know.

HANNAH   So that's it then.

DAVE   Yeah. 'Spose it is. Round 'ere they're bastards, Mum. Not all of 'em. Not my mates. But most of 'em. Show 'em any decency, you get shat on.

HANNAH   Yeah. What are we good for? Bastards like us? Poetry ain't for us. Kindness ain't for us. Violins ain't for us. Us bastards must be kept away from all things spiritual or sensitive. But that's the English in a way. God I love 'em really but... If those kids had been Irish they'd have respected your music.

DAVE   But Mum, these kids *were* Irish. Well, London-Irish anyway. O'Dowd, Healy, Downey, the lot of 'em.

HANNAH   Yeah. But would they have been like that had they stayed in Ireland? Perhaps. Still, your own tribe, eh? Shame. Your grandfather was a great fiddle player. Famous for it. Genius really. You couldn't even have that.

DAVE   How Irish am I Mum, anyway? Am I English? Irish? What?

HANNAH   How do you feel?

DAVE   I dunno. Never knew the English side of the family. Dad's side. Never met 'em. All the cousins and uncles and aunties were Irish. Feel closer to it, I suppose. When I hear that fiddle music I feel it in me guts. Love it. Understand it. At school I always felt a bit different from the English kids. I never felt – like I knew exactly where me guts were. Know what I mean?

HANNAH   I do, love.

DAVE   I 'spose I come over as English but me guts tell me somfin' else. All the 'thick paddy' jokes at school and the scraps me and the other London-Irish lads got into. But if I went to Ireland they'd think I was just another Brit, when really me heart's with them. Oh I dunno.

HANNAH   Would you ever want to go back there Dave?

DAVE   I used to love the holidays we had there. Creamy milk. Playing out late on the farm. That sort of –

light you get. *(beat)* Oh I dunno, Mum, I just feel funny, cooped up here. I'm old enough to have me own flat. But there ain't none. No job. No flat – I'm like a great big bleedin' baby. Still at home with me Mum and Dad.

HANNAH   You're wasted here, Dave. There's nothing for you here. Why don't you go somewhere where you could be happy? Why don't we both go back? Eh, Dave?

DAVE   I dunno, Mum.

HANNAH   Just the two of us. Or all of us. That would be best. *(quietly, or we hear Da's voice)* 'An Irish mother never leaves her family'. It's just a thing you get over here. The hatred. You see young men outside pubs. Looking at strangers with hatred. It's getting worse. There's a deadness here now. I always loved the English for a kind of tolerance they had. Mind you, it was tough when I first came over here. 'No blacks or Irish need apply' on ads for jobs or outside lodging houses. That shocked me, Dave.

DAVE   Yeah.

HANNAH   The joke was we all thought it was temporary. Said we'd be home soon. Lied to ourselves. We all stayed together, for protection, me and your uncles and aunts. Cricklewood, Kilburn, places like that. God, we worked hard. Just to survive. Sending a bit of money back home. But I always felt that the English were deep down in their hearts kind, strong people. The ones I met anyway. *(beat)* Things are changing, perhaps.

Da appears, seen only by Hannah.

DA   Han, have you told him of how Mr Cromwell took two hundred Irish women and children, herded them into a church, bolted the doors and set fire to it and over their screams, proclaimed he was doing the will of God?

HANNAH   Yes, I know that's true but I don't want to fill his mind with hate.

DAVE   Mum?

DA   History. Not hate for its own sake. What do you think his mind is full of now?

DAVE   Mum, what is it?

DA   Look at him. He comes from a line of warriors, chieftains and artists, and now his only joy and anger comes from hitting someone because they've spilled his beer or because they don't support the right football team. Eh? Where's the nobility in that? Where's the history, Han, where's the joy?

Lights change. In Hannah's view Dave changes into an ancient warrior.

DAVE   A young chieftain. A noble warrior.

HANNAH   My dangerous young prince.

DA   Ancient Hannah, bold and beautiful.

DAVE   My matriarch. My heroine. There's blood on these hands that serve you. A wind. A falcon rising. Our territory. Our patch. The filthy invaders closing on our hills, on our burial grounds, on our poetry and our fields, our souls.

HANNAH   You'd fight them with poetry if you could.

DAVE   If I could. But I live through this mud. Through this peat my fist comes punching up with a sword. To protect the soul of our land from the trees to the west and the bogs to the east.

DA   Directed energy. Applied. A noble soul. He's a good lad. A poet. A priest. A tree can't grow in a desert, Hannah.

Lights snap back to normal. Dave and Hannah alone again.

HANNAH *(cries out)* Da! I'm sorry, Da. I didn't mean to leave. I didn't want to give them this.

Dave is stunned. Holds Hannah.

DAVE   Mum. Oh God Mum what's going on, eh darlin'? What's the matter?

HANNAH   It's me Da, Dave. I keep thinking I see me Da.

DAVE   Mum.

HANNAH   He was here. He loves you. He says you could have been anything. Done anything. Do you believe me?

DAVE   Well –

HANNAH   Am I going mad, Dave?

DAVE   No, Mum. I believe you saw what you saw. *(holds her, rocks her.)* You feel a bit better now, love?

HANNAH *(tender, compassionate)* I'm sorry, Dave. I didn't want to bring you up around here. But it's all we settled for.

DAVE *(hugs her)* I love ya Mum. I do. *(They cuddle for a while.)*

HANNAH   See, love, I don't come from all this. When we were kids, we had space. We used to run barefoot along the fields to school in Ireland. Me and your uncles and aunts. We could do what we liked, laugh, scream, be ourselves.

DAVE   Yeah.

HANNAH   If there's a clear blue sky, I'll run today. They don't run with happiness. Anyone on this estate. It's all pretence and fear. They're like you, love. Running. Dodging through the flats. Scared. Scared of doing anything from sheer joy. Poor bastards.

DAVE   We're alright, though.

HANNAH   We could be. I just want to get outside all this for a while. Escape. Be selfish for once. Think about myself. *(Light)* Why don't you take me out, sometimes?

DAVE   Yeah. Where, though?

HANNAH   Oh, you know what I mean. Do something else.
The two of us. We can escape all of that round here. Me
and you. But, Dave I don't need anyone else. I can go on
my own.

DAVE   I'm with you Han. Eh?

HANNAH   What?

DAVE *(winks)* Fancy a pint?

HANNAH *(smiles)* Yeah.

Lights fade slowly.
The flat: *The sound of pop music on the radio. Sue sits at a*
table. She is getting ready to go out. She puts on make-up,
looking in a mirror. Hannah comes in, watches her. Sue hasn't
seen her. No words as Hannah watches. Finally Hannah leaves
without Sue noticing. Sue gets up. Music gets louder. She
dances in front of the mirror, turns to the audience. She is
ready.

SUE *(strong, defiant)* Right!

Music cuts. Blackout.
Spotlight: Hannah running through the estate.

HANNAH   The sky *is* blue. So I'm running. Look at it.
Sheer concrete. Shapes of steel lines of iron. Gaping slits
in blocks, flats, decks. Iron Gods. Old old shit. People here
dead. I'm running. This place is me. Designed by a fella.
Like to find the man who designed this place. People here
dead. No soul. No light. Just this. No one alive. Except for
me. Maybe I'm the last person alive in this place. People
here dead. *(pause)* I'm here. I'M AWAKE. I bleed. I can feel
blood. Body blood. Body-for-baby blood. I can still feel. I'm
here. YES, YOU. I'M HERE. No more rules. No more silent
sinking. Just me. I can see my face in concrete. My image.

My face concrete like me. So I'm running. *(She tears off her shoes, throws them in the air)* Ancient Celtic me. I'm in a RAGE with me. HERE I AM. Day after day of hiding. Year after year of anaemia. Throwing up in private. The polite smile. The reassuring hug. Denying myself any real PASSION. *(She starts ripping off her clothes)* But I'm still ALIVE. I made it. Maybe my prayers were heard. But, God, you've got to accept me as I am or lose me. 'Cos I'm going with or without you. I feel my SEX. JOY. WOMB. This is me, OK? This is me! *(She screams in triumph)*.

Blackout.
End of Act One.

ACT TWO

The flat: The room is blooming with flowers, in vases everywhere. Hannah is dressed in bright vivid colours. She wears lots of make-up. Her hair is down. Flowers in her hair. 'The folks who live on the hill' sung by Peggy Lee plays. Hannah moves to it, sings along. After a while, Ken arrives.

KEN   I got the wrong flat.

HANNAH   Beautiful, isn't it?

KEN   Oh, no.

HANNAH   Reminds me of beautiful places. Strangeness. Exotic smells. Adventures in far away lands. Blood colours. The red. Do you like it? That smell! I've been here. All day. Surrounded by them.

KEN   Yeah?

HANNAH   You used to love this song.

KEN   Yeah, well.

HANNAH   Let's get away somewhere, Ken. Sweep me off my feet to somewhere wonderful. Somewhere different. Just for a change.

KEN   Where?

HANNAH   Somewhere nice.

KEN   On my dole, do me a favour.

HANNAH   I've got a bit saved up.

KEN   Yeah, you won't have much of it left if you carry on taking days off and setting up as a florist.

HANNAH   Do you think I look nice?

KEN   Bit much, innit?

HANNAH   Yeah, I suppose so. But I want everything to be a bit much.

KEN   Do what?

HANNAH   I dunno. You know what I mean.

KEN   Yeah. *(pause)* Fancy going down the pub?

HANNAH   Can't you think of anything else? *(pause)* We could go to bed. Right now. Before the kids get back. *(She goes to him, he shrugs her off, slowly.)* Ken, I just need a bit of a cuddle, OK? *(He cuddles her.)* That's nice.

KEN   That enough?

HANNAH   Yeah. That was nice.

Ken sits down, gets paper out. Hannah takes it from him.

HANNAH   Come on, Ken. Let's go upstairs.

KEN   Don't wanna go upstairs.

HANNAH   Here then. Right here. Make love right here.

KEN *(embarrassed)* You been reading that pulp romance again?

HANNAH   I just *want* you. Know what I mean?

KEN   Don't feel like it love. *(takes paper back.)*

HANNAH   Why not? *(grabs paper out of his hand)*

KEN   Give it back.

HANNAH   I need you, you bastard.

KEN   I told you, I don't feel like it. Now give me the paper.

HANNAH   Oh yeah. *(turns to the pin-up on page 3)* Bet you'd feel like her, wouldn't you? If she came into this room now you'd feel like it.

KEN   Maybe – what's the matter with you today?

HANNAH   Well, how real do you think she is?

KEN   What's the matter?

HANNAH *(angry)* You are. I've got breasts as well, you know. But they're real and that's the problem ain't it?

KEN *(hard)* That's enough, OK? *(picks up paper and sits down. She turns the music off.)* You'd better get an early night. Don't want to miss another day.

HANNAH   I'm not going there again.

KEN   Oh yeah. I reckon.

HANNAH   I'm not going there again.

KEN   What you on about?

HANNAH   Time to throw in the towel. I've had enough.

KEN   We've been through all this before. You'll go in.

HANNAH   I won't.

KEN   How many more times do I have to tell you? Do yourself a favour, it's bad enough – me and Dave out of work – without you an' all. It's a disgrace when you've got a job.

HANNAH *(quiet)* A disgrace? Tens of thousands. Day in day out. On the treadmill. I can't believe I've made it this far. In my head. In my head there are a thousand pictures, without any story to 'em. They just go on. On the treadmill. Day in day out for hundreds of slow-moving years. So many corpses. Tens of thousands. Wasted bloody wreckage. I need to stand outside. See what's happening. A disgrace?

KEN   You *have* been reading them romances again.

HANNAH   Look, Ken. I just want some time to myself. I had a lovely day today.

KEN   Yeah, but how long do you think it'll last? When I was made redundant, the first month was like being on holiday. You've got to keep occupied, keep your mind occupied.

HANNAH   It is – occupied. I just want to – get to know about myself. Get to know you better. That's all I want.

KEN   You don't reckon thirty years is enough?

HANNAH   Yeah, but we've never spent much time together.

KEN   Look we had Sue and Dave to think about.

HANNAH   Those two are like strangers to us. Sue's out every night – where's her life going? What does she want from life?

KEN   Sue's OK. She's holding down a steady job. One day soon she'll get married. She'll be OK.

HANNAH   You think so?

KEN   I'll have a word with her.

HANNAH *(stares at Ken)* What about Dave? When was the last time you sat down and talked to him?

KEN   He's a bloody little vandal and that ain't down to me, neither.

HANNAH   You know he's not though, Ken.

KEN   What do you mean, I know he's not?

HANNAH   It's OK.

KEN   What about me? If you'd pay me a bit more attention instead of pampering them two – oh, why do I bother?

Lighting change. Hannah and Ken in their youth. Reprise of 'Folks who live on the hill'.

KEN   I've only known you a year, gel, but it just gets stronger, don't it?

HANNAH   Yes. It does. You look so handsome in that suit.

KEN   Yeah? Yeah. Not bad at all. Best worker on the line – best suits.

HANNAH	Showing off again, eh?
KEN	Course darlin.'
HANNAH	Love me?
KEN	Yeah. Course I do, Hannie. And you?
HANNAH	Very much darlin'.

KEN   Irish women. Beautiful. We're gonna be great. Us two. I can feel it. Change the bleeding' world. Oh 'scuse me French. Strong. That's how you make me feel. Could fight a bleedin' lion.

They kiss passionately. Lights fade. Music cuts.

HANNAH	Ken, I wanted to tell you something.
KEN	What?
HANNAH	I've see me Da.
KEN	Do what?
HANNAH	I've seen me Da. He appeared to me.
KEN	You – what – you –
HANNAH	In me head, maybe. I dunno. But I saw him.
KEN	Oh.
HANNAH	Well?
KEN	I – Are you OK?

HANNAH   I don't know. He said we should go back to Ireland, love. The family.

KEN   Look. You're tired. You been working too hard. Seen your Dad? Well...

HANNAH	Strange, isn't it? Ken, am I going mad?
KEN	I dunno. Nah. Not really. Ghost, was it?
HANNAH	I don't know.

KEN *(fascinated)* Cos I reckon they hang about, you know. Creepy, ain't it? I read about this bloke who went to Egypt. Reckons he saw all these old people, like from the olden days. Kings an' that. Where was he?

HANNAH   In the house.

KEN   Creepy, eh?

HANNAH   He told me to take the family back to Ireland.

KEN   Yeah, well.

HANNAH   But I've been thinking about it, anyway, Ken. I'm sick and tired of this place.

KEN   Yeah. I know.

HANNAH   You're always wanting to go abroad.

KEN   Yeah, but Ireland ain't abroad, is it? It's Britain.

(She bristles, does not want to argue)

HANNAH   I want to go, Ken.

KEN   Don't be silly, love.

HANNAH   I'm not being silly. I just want to go home. Me and you could have a bit more space. Get closer.

KEN   I dunno.

HANNAH   Look. I'd like to go with you and the kids but I'll go on my own if necessary.

KEN   Nah, you won't. You won't leave. That's the one thing about you Irish women. My Dad said that. He said, 'You want yer head examined but you got a good sort there'.

HANNAH   I want to go home, Ken.

KEN   Look. Take a bit o' time. Think it over.

HANNAH   I have done.

KEN   Thanks for telling me first.

HANNAH   I tried to. I wanted to.

KEN   What would we do out in Ireland? I mean, they ain't – sort of, my type of people.

HANNAH   Why not?

KEN   Argumentative. Violent. Horrible place. There's no work, neither.

HANNAH   I'm sure you'd find something. Is there any work for you here?

KEN   No, but it's what I know, ain't it?

HANNAH   What you know? What about all those adventures you want to go on?

KEN   I will. One day. But I don't see sitting in a pub in the middle of a bog on a rainy day as adventure.

HANNAH   I want to go Ken.

KEN *(snaps)* Well you go then. I'm staying here. And the kids. That's that. *(She goes to him and tries to put her arms around him. He moves away.)*

HANNAH *(angry)* Look, you bastard, am I that disgusting?

KEN *(hard, snaps, displacement)* Yeah. What's the matter with you? Ghosts and Ireland and sex mad. What's the fucking problem, eh?

HANNAH *(quiet rage)* I'm not disgusting.

KEN   Look.

HANNAH *(frenzy building)* I'm not disgusting, I'm not disgusting. I'm not disgusting.

KEN   For fuck's sake -

HANNAH *(screaming)* Not disgusting! Not disgusting! *(She starts to attack him. He slaps her really hard across the face. She stops. Pause, quietly)* Thank you. I'm not disgusting.

Ken walks slowly, calmly, out. Hannah just sits there. She takes the flower out of her hair, empties all the flower vases, puts on 'Mna na Heirreann' (Women of Ireland) by the Chieftains. She sits there, bites off the head of a flower, eats it, crying. Lights fade.

<u>Ritual Tableaux:</u> *We see a repeat of the kitchen ritual we saw earlier. This time Sue is holding the plates, etc. Dave and Ken sitting at the table. Hannah's chair empty. Lights change. Then Dave running through streets. The actor runs on the spot.*

DAVE   Oi! You seen my Mum? My *Mum*. Mum. Mum. Where? Mum. Where are you Mum. Name. Han. Han. *Han!*

I fucking need ya. Mum! Please come back. I need ya. Mum. *Han!*

Lights change. Ken in a pub, holding a pint of bitter. Very drunk, thinking.

KEN   Gone. Finally gone. Gone off her head. Funny lot, the Irish. Two bleedin' days of Sue's cooking. Not that I mind cooking. When she was ill that time I cooked and helped out with the washing up. Then when I told her I'd done it, she said, 'Why can't you just do it without asking for a medal?' I don't half pick 'em. *(beat)* She was a looker, though. Beautiful. Diamond of a girl. Proud to take her out, I was. I don't know. It'll all blow over. Clear itself up. We had a laugh, though. Battersea funfair. The Cat's Whiskers, the Lyceum. Good job, then. Now no one'll employ ya if you're over the age of six. This beer's piss. They do that, don't they? In the desert. Drink piss. Filtered by the sand. *(pause)* I wouldn't mind going there. The desert. Just to see it. *(suddenly bitter, desperate)* Fuckin' in one, ain't I? *(regains control)* Wouldn't catch me drinking piss, though. *(looks at his glass).*

Sue enters with a drink.

SUE   Alright, Dad? *(He gives her a kiss)*
KEN   Hello gorgeous, had a good day?
SUE *(concerned)* You had a few then, Dad? Take it easy eh? *(He nods. Bright)* Yeah, not too bad. That bitch of a supervisor, though. I think I just might knock her out one of these days.
KEN   Yeah?
SUE   Yeah, she's such a tight-arsed bitch. She came in today, looking like a right brass. How she's running a cosmetics department, I'll never know. She goes to me,

'We'll have a little less make-up please Sue'. A little less make-up? If she wore one more false eyelash she'd keel over. My life.

KEN   Yeah, I see her when I went in there. I goes, 'Can I speak to Sue, please?' She goes, 'Who?' I said 'I know it's not long but she *has* been working here four years, now. *(They try to laugh)*

SUE   Yeah, that's the one. She don't like me. Bloke she's got! Reckons he's all sun-tanned, but it's straight out of a bottle. Looks like he's smeared his face with baboon's afterbirth.

KEN   Hold up, Sue, it don't take much to put me off this little brew.

SUE   Yeah.

Blackout.
Then spotlight on Ken.

KEN *(thinking)* I think I'll go on a wine-tasting holiday in the Dordogne.

Lights snap back to normal.

SUE   Can I have a drop?
KEN   Yeah. *(hands her the glass)*
SUE *(disgust)* Oh, what? Tastes like a snake's arse.
KEN   Yeah.

Blackout.
Then spotlight on Sue.

SUE *(thinking)* This'll go on for a while. The same old jokes and chat. Look at him, though. Trying to ignore the fact that Mum's gone. He can't handle emotion. Can't talk about

it. He ain't a bad bloke. He's just, well... he's just a loser.
Let's face it. I can stand here and have a chat with him.
Have the odd laugh. But it ain't what I'm thinking. I'm
thinking, 'Why can't you get yourself a job, you old sod?'
Not nasty. Just sort of – real. I'm thinking what a randy old
bastard he is an' all. I see him in here sometimes. Eyeing
up the talent. No time for Mum like that. Don't blame her
for leaving really. Yeah, real lechy. Noncey stares across
the room. Mind you, some of 'em encourage him. Tease
him to get a drink. Slags. I don't tease no one. If I want to
have someone I have 'em. Simple as that. Go to clubs, see
a geezer – have a laugh. Marriage? Forget it. For now. I'm
also thinking about Mum – how she's ended up. But she
knew what she was doing. I ain't gonna end up like her. If
and when I marry it'll be someone rich and good-looking.
In that order. And sexy. You know what frightens me? I am
my Mum. I am, though. 'S I get older. I can see it. Little
things. Little habits. That's scary. But not just that. It's the
way me mind works, me ideas. Just like hers. Sometimes.
I can't explain it. But I can feel it. I'm becoming my Mum.
More and more each day. I love me family but... I dunno...
I just don't like 'em. I don't really know 'em. Can't – contact
'em. None of 'em. When I see the wallies on this estate and
in this pub I want to puke. I'll save up enough cash to get
away somewhere. In the sun. I'll send the odd postcard.
Then I won't have to be here. Thinking this.

Lights snap back to normal.

SUE   Hot in here, ain't it?
KEN   Certainly is, love.
SUE *(finally)* Look, Dad. What about Mum?
KEN *(bitter, internal)* Bitch.
SUE   Where do you reckon she is?
KEN   Dunno. Don't care.

SUE   Don't worry, Dad. She'll be back.

KEN   Don't want her back.

SUE   What about her side?

KEN *(loud, painful)* Her side? Her fuckin' side?

SUE   Quiet, Dad. She's just going through a bad
patch. I dunno. She might need some of them – what do
you call 'em? Valium. Tranquillisers. Help her through it.
You should get her to see the doctor, Dad.

KEN   D'ya reckon?

SUE   Yeah. 'Snothing serious. Lot of people take 'em,
you know. I bet there's a lot of 'em in this place, right now.
Take away the tranquillisers and the whole world would
just crack up.

KEN   One big breakdown, you mean.

SUE   Thassit. One big breakdown. Anyway, Dad.
Must be going.

KEN   Going out?

SUE   Yeah. Club.

KEN   See ya love. *(He kisses her cheek, runs his
hand slowly through her hair. Hold the moment.)*

SUE *(moves away)* Bye, Dad. Don't worry, eh?

She goes.

KEN *(To himself)* One big breakdown.

Lights fade.
*Top of block of flats: Moonlight. Hannah stands with her
suitcase, alone.*

HANNAH   So this is it. Top of the highest tower block.
Instone Close. Made it. Right near the edge. *(pause)* Long
way down. Long way to fall. Fallen. Fallen. Oh God, fallen.
(She stands at the edge, about to throw herself off.)

Out of the darkness, a figure appears. He is dressed in full bishop's vestments in green, complete with mitre. In one hand he holds a cigarette, in the other a pint of Guinness.

FIGURE *(broad Dublin accent)* Now then, Han. What's all the fuss?

HANNAH   Who the hell are you?

PATRICK   Language. Anyway, you can't get Guinness in hell.

HANNAH   Whoever you are, just leave me alone.

PATRICK   I can't leave you alone. You prayed to me.

HANNAH *(amazement)* Patrick? Oh no. No.

PATRICK   Saint Patrick if you please. Me mates call me Paddy.

HANNAH   Oh leave me alone, will you? I can't take this. You're not real. I can't take this. I don't believe you're here.

PATRICK   Don't be such an ungrateful gob-shite I've come a long way to be here.

HANNAH   Where from?

PATRICK   Football match at Croke Park. Hill Sixteen. Me favourite spot. We was winning too. The guv'nor dragged me away. Emergency, he says. So what's the problem?

HANNAH   Look, this is a very special, serious moment in my life. Delicate. Important. Don't cheapen it with your stupid version of Irish whimsy.

PATRICK   Don't be a bollix. I'm a bleedin' apparition. I'm entitled to be whimsical.

HANNAH   That's it.

PATRICK   Wait, Han. Wait, will ya? I'm sorry. It's just me way. You don't get to convert the Irish by being a wimp. Look, I'm a Saint, right? I exist, whether you like it or not and I know that you've got yer old man and a coupla kids back down there who love ya. Right? You've gotta take 'em

to Ireland or stay here. Leaving on your own or jumping
over just aren't the way.

HANNAH   Why not?

PATRICK   Do you want to spend eternity without
Guinness or music or laughter or a fag or two?

HANNAH   *Go away!*

PATRICK   Besides. You're an Irish woman.

HANNAH   Yeah? So? What *is* that? What does that mean?
It's like a band of death around my neck. 'Irish Woman'. Is
that English for 'Not free'? Is that man's talk for 'Not free'?

PATRICK   Not much freedom in being splattered among
the shite and fish and chip wreckage down there.

HANNAH   Yes there is, Paddy. Yes there is.

PATRICK   What?

HANNAH *(calm, serenity)* Coldness. Blackness. Death. No
ideas. No worries. Not existing. Thin. Empty. Gone.
Forever. A brief spark. Then gone. Nothingness. Beautiful.

PATRICK   Han, stop for God's sake. You know that's not
true.

HANNAH   Do I?

PATRICK   Yeah. It's not over when you breeze out, you
know. I can tell ya.

HANNAH   What is it then?

PATRICK   Secret. *(quickly, to Hannah's reaction)* But I will
say this. It's not just the old bollix of reward and punishment. That's part of it but – I dunno – it's more an –
easiness in space. A light. An energy. Don't do it, Han, love.
Hang on in there. Will ya? Look, someone's coming. I better
go.

HANNAH *(looking round)* Who?

PATRICK   Dunno. *(leaving)* Han?

HANNAH   What?

PATRICK   You're alright, you know that?

HANNAH   Yeah?

PATRICK   Yeah. See yiz.

He disappears. Hannah stands on her own. Dave arrives on the roof.

DAVE   Mum. Hannah. What you doing up here?

HANNAH   Hello, Dave.

DAVE   God, Mum, I've been so worried about you. Where've you been?

HANNAH   Walking around. Thinking. *(He goes to her)* Don't, Dave. Don't come too close.

DAVE   Mum, be careful.

HANNAH   Just surveying our little kingdom.

DAVE   Get away from the edge, Mum.

HANNAH   No.

DAVE   Come on.

HANNAH   Please, Dave. Leave me alone. I have to be alone to do this.

DAVE   Oh, what? Come down, Mum.

HANNAH   Please, Dave. I don't want you to see it.

DAVE   Mum. I been thinking. What you were saying. 'Bout Ireland. You gotta go.

HANNAH   Too late, love.

DAVE   No. You go. Go on. You're too good for this place. Go back to Ireland.

HANNAH   I *can't*. Not now.

DAVE   Why not?

HANNAH   Makes you feel like God or something. Looking down. Look, there's our flat. Looks so small. It's like Jesus on the mountain. The devil appears to tempt him. 'If you throw yourself down you will be caught by angels'.

DAVE   Not many angels round here.

HANNAH   Some. Some. Would *I* be caught, I wonder? How far would I fall? I've already done it though, Dave. I thought your father was an angel.

DAVE *(pause)* Have you see Da again, Mum?

HANNAH No. Not much. I think he's left me.

DAVE   Maybe he said all he had to say.

HANNAH   Yeah.

DAVE *(moving to her)* Look, Mum -

HANNAH   *Don't. (he stops)* I just don't have the nerve, Dave. Going back to Ireland on my own. Deserting the family. It goes against my guts, everything I've been taught to believe a mother should do.

DAVE   None of us deserve you, Mum. Dad doesn't. Sue doesn't. Just go. Just be free for once in your life.

HANNAH   I can't Dave. I haven't got the courage.

DAVE *(desperate)* Well why don't you come back home, then? Try and make a go of it here. We'll go out together, do things together like you said.

HANNAH   Dave. I can't come home.

DAVE   You can't come home, you can't go to Ireland. What...?

HANNAH   *I can go down.* Down. Descend into hell. I can't stay. I can't leave. But I can go down.

DAVE   Mum. For God's sake. I love you darlin.' Mum... You mean more to me than anything or anyone else in the whole fuckin' world. Don't that mean nothing to you?

HANNAH *(exploding, building, intense) Yes!* You bloody little fool. Yes it does. Love? Love got me up here. Love? It's a dark golden burning lucifer of coldness with a fiery burning halo disguising it. Love. Love destroys it's own children. Love hammers people to crosses. Love burns down houses. *Love?* Unless you're standing here on the edge with me don't talk to me about love. It's ugly and cruel... and... and I don't want to live in a world where there are... no lions anymore... The grief of it... God – the death and sex and horror of it all. We're burning down the world with love. We're pouring filth into the sky with love. I eat love. The love that hurts. That blinded that Paul fella on the road. The love that wounds... Wounded healer. Don't talk to me about love, boy, man, fooleen, gossoon. Turn me skull inside out with it. Lord God punish me with love. *(screams to the world)* Hello everyone down there. I'm Hannah and my skull is exploding with love and pain and guilt and purity. I'm alive and I'm in pain and I'm sad. There! Lord I hate you and love you. I'm losing my faith. Lost it perhaps. But I must believe. I must allow myself to believe. There must be more to life than this. Than that down there. The ripped-up buses, the greed, the shopping trolleys, the hatred, the violence, the graffiti, the sheer grey numbness of it. *(suddenly calm, quiet.)* Up here. Quiet. You can't hear their pain. But it's there. Private. Locked up. *(looks at Dave)* Dave. If I went to Ireland. Would you come with me?

DAVE   I dunno, darlin.'

HANNAH   What?

DAVE *(almost crying)* I ain't gonna say yes I'll go to stop you jumping. I ain't gonna lie to you. Not now, Mum. I just need more time. You've got to make a decision here. You've got to make your own choice. And I'm tellin' ya. I love ya. I don't know what that means but I know I feel it in me guts. That's it.

HANNAH *(quiet, still)* A Heroic Decision. Yeah. That's about it. *(pause. She thinks)* Dave, you believe in me, don't you?

DAVE   Yeah. Course I do.

HANNAH *(simply)* I'm going home, Dave.

Dave rushes up to her. They hug. Dave cries. A little boy. Hard man gone. They go slowly downstairs. Lights fade.

The flat: Ken sitting down, tipsy, with a bunch of flowers on his lap. 'Folks who live on the hill' playing. Ken sings along with it.

KEN Fuckin' foreigner. At the bar. Started pushin' me. I asked him politely enough. 'Oi, fucker, hold up will you?' He took a swipe at me. *(suddenly vulnerable)* Han... Han... Her eyes. Miss 'em...Voice. Sound of her coming in the door. Her nuttiness. Miss it. Too much time to think. Looking at meself. Grey, kind of thing. Useless. Redundant. Sound of her snoring. Even miss that. Way she coughs a little bit during the night. Way her nose goes. *(desperate, pain)* I need ya, Han. *(controlled)* No. *(pain)* I need ya darlin.' *(hard again)* I blocked it with me left and clumped him with me right. Like the old days. Still pretty fit. So he's on the deck. 'Had enough, boy?' 'Yeah', he goes. Well it ain't right to go on. Not like the kids now. Booting someone when he's on the deck. Having people over from behind with blades and all that. Like that Dave. Reckons he's the real hard man. We could have shown him a thing or two. The Bermondsey boys. Now *they* were hard. Cruel but fair. There was Johnny the head case, Sam and Joe the blade brothers, Frank, the one-eyed Irishman with a right so hard they had him deported. Yeah. Good geezers. We had a code. There were rules of the game. Now they've all gone fucking mad. You could go out of a day – leave the door open – nothing got nicked. You never nicked from one of your own. Now they don't give a fuck for no one. No one.

Sue enters.

SUE Hello Dad. How are ya?
KEN Well, I had to turn down the invitation to Highgrove from the Prince of Wales. Camilla was a bit put out and the Sultan of Brunei ain't feelin' too good neither. Other than that it's been a quiet evening.

SUE   Flowers?

KEN   Yeah. She phoned. Said she might come and pick up the rest of her things. Thought I might – you know.

SUE   Yeah. Where's Dave?

KEN   Still out looking for her. Takes after her, he does. Right pair of nutters. Still, maybe once she got them pills she'd calm down a bit, eh?

SUE   Yeah.

KEN *(pause)* Have a good night?

SUE   Not too bad. You been in all night?

KEN   Yeah. Well – after the pub closed.

SUE   You eaten?

KEN   Yeah. Pub grub. *(pause)* Sue, what happened to that bloke you was going out with?

SUE   Which one?

KEN   Nice geezer – one I saw in the pub.

SUE   Gary – oh I blew him out.

KEN   Why?

SUE   Bad breath.

KEN   Bad breath? You blew him out 'cos he had bad breath?

SUE   Yeah.

KEN   He seemed like a nice enough geezer to me.

SUE   He was alright. I just got bored.

KEN   Listen, love. You know, you've gotta start thinking about finding a fella.

SUE   Why?

KEN   All this to-ing and fro-ing.

SUE   Look Dad, I've got time.

KEN   Listen, my love. *I'd* have swept you off your feet as soon as look at ya.

SUE   Ta. But look, I'm alright.

KEN   Well, I'm telling you. Your youth ain't gonna last forever. It's like a greyhound at Walthamstow. You see it all lovely and glistening ready to go with its coat on and freshly painted number. The roar of the crowd. They're expecting something. Then the hare runs, the trap flies up and it's gone. Along with a load of lost bets.

SUE   I ain't a bleedin' greyhound. I know what I'm doing. I got time. *(pause. She feels like telling him)* When I see this place and the people in it I could throw up. I mean it. I don't want fish and chips and a mini-cab home after the club forever. I dunno, I just reckon there's something else. I don't wanna be leered at. I don't wanna be treated like a bit of meat, but I am. That's the way it is. So that's the way I treat blokes, Dad. Meat. Some steak, some Kangaroo burger.

KEN   What about love, gel?

SUE *(gentle)* Come on, Dad.

KEN   Yeah.

SUE   Look, Dad, that's it though. I'm happy enough. I just ain't staying here.

KEN   Do me a favour, girl. I never said you should. You're sounding like your mother.

SUE *(firm)* No. Not like that. Not her way. *(pause)* I seen photographs of you when you was younger. You were a good looking bloke.

KEN *(light)* What's all this 'were' business?

SUE   No, you know what I mean.

KEN   Yeah, but so was your Mum.

SUE   Yeah, but she was stupid.

KEN   Hold up.

SUE   She was, Dad. She took what she was offered. You and the whole thing and bought it. All I'm saying is I'm gonna take me time. Wait for the right opportunity, that's all. *(pause)*

KEN *(smiles)* Well, if you're sure, Sue. Stone me you've always had your head screwed on.

He gets up, puts record on. Smoochy number. He dances round the room.

KEN   Come on, Sue.
SUE   Nah.
KEN   Come on. Make out I'm some sharp geezer in an I-tie whistle.
SUE   Oh, alright. *(She joins him. He holds her at some distance)* Dad, you ain't a bad little mover.
KEN   In my day, girl. In my day.

Sudden spotlight on Ken. Music sharp, pounding and hard. Suddenly he seems thirty years younger.

KEN   In my day we could have shit 'em. There's a beautiful girl on yer arm and a sparkle in yer eye. A cool clean feeling washing up yer back like millions of little needles o' fun. You feel good. You look good. Yer with your mates. You stroll up to the bar. Anyone looks at yer lady, you lay 'em out. It's a feeling in the gut. Like the dark in the building and the lights on the dance floor. It's real and it's old and you know you're YOUNG. It's the looks of admiration on yer mates' faces. Just a glint, a nod or a stare. She was a good dancer, too. Stockings, high heels. Fresh face. Nose, eyes, everything right. You got a job, you got mates, you got money and the evening's never gonna stop with booze and the music pounding and lifting ya. You can't see *this* moment. Not the here and now of it. Not the blood and pain and failure and heartache and dead old bones of it. Cos you're YOUNG.

Lights snap back to normal. Ken moves closer to Sue. Sensual. They move together. He lifts his hand and strokes Sue's hair. Hannah and Dave enter. Hannah stares at Ken. Sue and Ken break off. Silence. Embarrassment.

KEN   Oh. Hello. Been doing some dancing. Just teaching Sue the Old Style.

HANNAH   The Old Style?

KEN   Where you been or am I allowed to ask?

HANNAH   Around. I've been out with Dave.

KEN   What you doing keeping your Mum out all night?

DAVE *(glares)* We felt like it.

KEN   Don't get lippy with me, son.

HANNAH *(pause)* So.

KEN   Yeah.

HANNAH   Anyway.

KEN   Look, Han. Can we talk?

HANNAH *(gentle)* No, Ken. I've just come for the rest of my things. I'm going home.

KEN   This is your home, love.

HANNAH   Really?

KEN   Look, can we talk alone?

HANNAH   No, Ken.

KEN   Come on.

HANNAH *(calm)* I'll just get the rest of my things. Sorry, love. *(She goes to the door. Ken takes her arm)*

KEN   Look, Han. *(embarrassed at Sue and Dave being there, standing uncomfortably)* I – I been thinking. I need you here.

HANNAH   Ken, please.

KEN   You can't go, Han. Please.

HANNAH   Ken -

KEN *(with difficulty, costs him a lot)* You wanted me. Right? You wanted me. Yeah. I shoulda said this before. Couldn't. Anyway. You wanted a man. I'd had me balls cut off when I was made redundant. No pride. When it first happened you were so bleedin' kind to me. Kindness, yeah. Then pity. I couldn't. Couldn't see meself as a man. No pride. No. Got worse and worse. Lost interest in it. Didn't – deserve it.

HANNAH   Kenny...

KEN   Kind to me. You was, Han. I'm in fuckin' hell. Right now. You gotta help me. You gotta be kind to me again. Just a little bit. Please stay, Han.

HANNAH   I can't, Ken. I can't. Not now.

KEN *(panic, fear, anger)* You fuckin' bitch. What I done. Yeah. What I done for you. Wasted me life on you. When I was working it was OK, weren't it? Oh yeah. OK then. Now I'm out, you're done with me, ain't ya? I hate you. *(He slaps her really hard across the face. Dave starts to go for him.)*

HANNAH   Don't Dave! *(He stops, goes to comfort Hannah.)*

KEN   Han, I'm sorry.

SUE *(finally cracking)* You fucking old cow! *(She shouts through tears)* Just kick him while he's down, why don't you? Why don't you just fuck off if you feel so bad about it here? Go on. I've had enough of all this moaning and weird chat. Giving everyone a hard time. You made your choice with Dad and us so you can bloody well take the consequences.

HANNAH   I made my bed. But I can remake it. I don't have to lie in it.

SUE   Oh. Piss off then. I don't care. You either stay here and stop moaning – like me – or you should just piss off.

HANNAH   Sue, I didn't know. I didn't. Life is something that just crept up on me. OK? I couldn't plan it.

SUE   Well, I can.

HANNAH   How different do you think it'll be?

SUE   Act your age. That's the trouble though, ain't it? It's all going and you can't handle it.

DAVE   Fuckin' 'ell Sue.

SUE   She's old enough to know better. I want something, Mum. OK? Something better.

HANNAH   Great. So do something about it.

SUE   I will, but I ain't gonna do what you did.

HANNAH   I'm glad.

SUE   You ain't got a clue, have you?

DAVE   Knock it on the head, OK?

SUE   I've just about had enough of this.

DAVE   Oh yeah? Gettin' fed up with the cooking are ya?

SUE   Yeah, right.

DAVE   Now you know what it feels like, don't ya?

SUE   Oh yeah, why don't you do some fuckin' work round here.

DAVE   Look at him. (Ken) He ain't done a stroke round 'ere.

KEN   That's enough, Dave.

DAVE *(to Ken)* Button it, wanker. *(To Sue)* Just 'cos he ain't workin' don't mean he can treat Mum like a fuckin' slave.

KEN *(to Hannah)* Did you fill his head with this?

DAVE *(to Ken)* One reason. Go on. One good reason why you should lounge around while Mum's working and expect three meals a day.

KEN   Watch it, Dave.

DAVE   One reason. *(pause)* There ain't none. You two have got some front. You can't see her, can you? Can't see what she is. Well, I shit on ya. I shit on you and yourn. You're right, Han. There's nothing for us here. I'm comin' with ya.

HANNAH   Dave –

DAVE   But first. On your feet Dad. We're going for a walk upstairs. Right to the top of the block.

KEN   What you on about?

DAVE   Get moving. *(glares)* I wanna talk to you. *(Ken senses he has no choice)*

HANNAH   What are you doing?

DAVE   Bastards, Mum. I told ya, didn't I? Bastards.
(Ken goes with Dave, clutching the flowers.)

DAVE   See you in a while, Han.

HANNAH   Where are you going?

They leave. Uncomfortable silence between Sue and Hannah.

SUE *(finally)* What's Dave gonna do? He won't hurt Dad, will he?

HANNAH   No, love.
(Silence. They stare at each other. They move slowly towards each other. Hannah strokes Sue's hair.) Strangers.

SUE   Yeah.

HANNAH *(gently)* Do you really hate me, Sue?

SUE *(quiet)* No. Don't like you very much. Can't lie about that.

HANNAH   I know love. *(Sue puts her arms round Hannah)*

SUE *(very quietly)* Love ya, though.

HANNAH *(smiles, rocks Sue)* So this is it. The funny thing was I knew it would come to this. Deep inside me. Selling myself short. It was like a novelty, I suppose. Self-destruction, cheapening myself. You're right, Sue. It *is* all going. But it's not too late. I've got to get out, love. If you ignore reality for too long, it'll kick you in the head for attention. I'm leaving, Sue. Tonight.

SUE *(beat)* Best a' luck Mum.

Lights fade slowly.

Rooftop: _Moonlight. The top of the block._

DAVE   Can you see it Dad?

KEN   What you dragging me up here for?

DAVE   Can you see it?

KEN   Yeah. Got vertigo.

DAVE   Well ain't it lovely? This is what we've got. Couple of bastards like me and you. S'all we need.

KEN   Look, stop pissing about, Dave.

DAVE   Bottle ain't going is it, Dad? I thought we were the Real Men – me and you.

KEN _(scared)_ You're fuckin' mad.

DAVE   Yeah. Maybe I am. I don't give a shit for you, this place. Where's your stories now Dad? Where's your big stories about how you took five on single-handed. In your day? How about taking _this_ place on?

KEN   Let's go down now shall we?

Dave spits. Watches it go sailing down.

DAVE   Long way down ain't it Dad?

KEN   Yeah.

DAVE   Quickest way down, though. Right. To the edge, sunbeam.

KEN   No.

DAVE _(pushes him)_ To the edge. Now on your knees.

KEN   No.

DAVE   On your knees. _(Ken kneels down, terrified, at the edge.)_ You need this, Dad. I'm gonna show you the kingdom. Right. Beautiful, ain't it? This is where you live. This is where you brought me up. You ain't going nowhere but here. 'Less you change. This is it for you. End of the line time. There ain't no package tours to Tunisia, Nairobi, China or fuck all anywhere else. _Got it?_ I'm half your age and I can see that. I've accepted it. I know we got fuck all now but I'm gonna do something about it. I'm out of here. This is your lot, Ken. This is what you settled for.

KEN   No, no.

DAVE   Right. Why couldn't you have told Mum what you was feeling before? Eh? 'Hard Man'? Is that it? Afraid? Yeah. Me too. Dead similar. Me and you. Dreams is good. But not bullshit ones. You gotta see that. I want you to see that, Dad. Otherwise you'll dream yourself up your own arse and snuff it there. Have a good butchers at reality, Dad. Like Mum done. Like I done. Then maybe you just might have a chance.

KEN   Alright, I promise. *(pause)*

DAVE *(quiet)* It's so still. Up here. No sound. Funny. Everyone quiet for once. Quietly sleeping. No nothing from no one. Like none of them give a shit. She's right, you know. Han. They've accepted it. Most of 'em. Settled for it. But you got something, Dad. We don't get on or nothing but I can see... you're... deep down... you're alright.

KEN   You reckon, Dave?

DAVE   I know it, you old sod. Alright, Ken. Get up. *(Ken gets up. He vomits.)* That's right, Dad. Get it all out of your system.

KEN   Can I go down now?

DAVE   Yeah. You–can–go–down–now.

Ken walks slowly away. Hannah arrives. Ken passes her. Stops. Gives her the bunch of flowers.

KEN   I–bought–you–some–flowers.

Hannah smiles, takes them. A moment between them in which we feel they want to say something to each other. Ken kisses her lightly on the cheek, leaves. Hannah looks at the flowers.

HANNAH   So.
DAVE   So.
HANNAH   Nervous?
DAVE   Yeah.
HANNAH   Me too.

We hear an air on the fiddle. Wind blowing.

HANNAH   Dave, Da's here. He's come back.
DAVE   I know. I felt it.
HANNAH   I'm coming home, Da.

The sound of the wind starts to build. Dave and Hannah blown by it, struggle to hold on.

HANNAH *(pointing)* Look. That's the direction of Ireland.
DAVE   Yeah. Yeah.
HANNAH   I'm coming home, Da. I'm coming home.

Sound of wind blowing hard now, mixed with the plaintiff fiddle air. Hannah has to shout above it. She throws the flowers into a shower in the air. Petals fall.

HANNAH   One two three – who'll remember me? Five six seven – I'm on my way to heaven.

The sounds of the wind and the fiddle build to a loud climax. Sound and lights snap off.

The end.

Fall From Light

Originally commissioned by Manchester Royal Exchange Theatre.

CHARACTERS
Deborah
Jeremy
Simon
Girly
Shrimpdick
Velvetblade
Mr Smith
Old Blind Man *can double with*
Security Guard/Priest/Voice of Interviewer

SCENE ONE
Spotlight up on the Opera House Director, Jeremy Wonfrey.
He is in a frenzy of inspiration.

JEREMY   The function of Art. The nature of Art.
The purpose of Art is to give us a flash of heaven.
A glimpse. Through a glass darkly.
To lift us from the blather of the ordinary.
To bathe us in the light of the eternal.
To drag us from the primeval bog of the valley and up
To the Mountains of the Gods.
To breathe the same vivifying air as the Gods.
(pause)
And the greatest of the arts is opera. The impossible art...
Music...
Theatre...

Music Theatre. The spoken word. The sung word.
Dithyrambic. Atavistic voices. Design. Acting. The orchestra.
All coming. Together. All reaching a synthesis. All coming
together.
A Gesamtkunstwerk.
A Total Art Work.
But the madness of it all. People singing to each other
What is normally spoken.
Ludicrous. Unnatural. Supernatural.
Why should we believe it? Well some stories are so sublime
They must be sung. The race memory of these islands.
The Bardic tradition.
Using all these different elements.
Each magically potent on its own.
But together.
Together the heavens are breached.
We are transformed from the clay of our mortal selves
Into the eternal, the heavenly.
In a form that we can see. We can see this heaven.
Right here on earth. *(pause)*
A pathetic prosaic reed is turned, by blowing,
Into the tool of the Zephyr.
This weakness of the flesh inspired by the breathing of art
Into the songs of the angels.
And we can see this.
And we can feel this.
And we can have this.
Right here. Right here.
On this Earth.
An intimation, a glimpse of Heaven!

*He shouts in pleasure. The lighting widens to show he is in
bed. From under the covers comes Deborah Mullins, a rising
young diva.*

DEBORAH   Yeah?

JEREMY   Yes. As perfect as your singing.

DEBORAH   Yeah?

JEREMY   I always loved your tongue technique.

DEBORAH   And my breath control?

JEREMY   Oh yes. Superlative.

DEBORAH   My turn. *(lies back. Jeremy goes under the covers)* Here I am. Is this happening? All this. I'm singing the roles I always wanted. Aaaah. I'm with you. I can't believe it. Aaaah. I'm going to admit something to you. Ooooh. I fancied you when I first saw you. Yes. As a student. Down a bit. Yes. We'd come to a dress rehearsal. Ah. You were just The Boss to me then. You were in the auditorium. Shouting at the director. Mmmm. Ooooh. Then the usual bullshit. The right agent. The right dinner parties. But if I hadn't met you at that dinner party at ...oooh ....where was it?

JEREMY *(looking up)* Lord Turlington's. *(goes back)*

DEBORAH   Yes. He was lovely too. The Chairman. What was the old joke about him? Oh yes. What's the difference between a toddler and Lord Turlington? Well, a toddler sucks his fingers and Lord Turlington...

JEREMY *(looking up)* Fucks his singers?

DEBORAH   Correct.

JEREMY   Did he –?

DEBORAH   Of course.

JEREMY   Really?

DEBORAH   Yes.

JEREMY   When?

DEBORAH   That night. In the grounds. *(He resumes his business)* He put down his cohiba and pulled up my dress. His mouth tasted of cigars, decay and port. Gorgeous. Mmm... Mmmm... So you see, it's really empirical evidence to suggest that the old cliché is true. It's not what you

know... oooh oooooh aaa aaah, it's... oooh, it's... oooh, it's...
(She climaxes. Pause)

JEREMY *(looking up)* Cup of tea?
DEBORAH   Lovely.

Blackout.

SCENE 2

Eden Housing Estate. Near the Docks. Night. Very loud guitar music cuts through the dark. The lights come up on four young men – the gang. We see Girly, Mr Smith, Velvetblade and Shrimpdick run on. High on adrenalin and speed. They stare out at us. Victorious.

MR SMITH   We skinned 'em!

VELVETBLADE   We done 'em!

SHRIMPDICK   We flattened 'em!

GIRLY   I striped the big geezer's face.

SHRIMPDICK   Reckoned they could take our block.

VELVETBLADE   I got 'old of Dave's head. I smashed it through a plate glass window.

SHRIMPDICK   I chased two of 'em into the chip shop. I slashed one of 'em and put the other cunt's head into the deep fryer.

MR SMITH   I held Big Phil's head down. Then I smashed it open. Sweet.

SHRIMPDICK   Girly's was the best.

MR SMITH   Yeah. He done three of 'em.

VELVETBLADE   Sweet as a nut, that was.

SHRIMPDICK   How'd it go, Girly?

GIRLY   One of 'em had a chopper. He's gone "Do you want some, cunt?" I've gone "Yeah". I nutted him, got the chopper out of his hand and hacked both his fuckin' shins.

VELVETBLADE He's a fuckin' artist, he is. What 'bout the other one?

GIRLY   He come at me with a broken bottle. He's gone "You reckon?" I just put the fuckin' axe in his head. Then the last one, Steve. Smelly Steve from the next block? Well, he's got a baseball bat and a chain. He's swung the baseball bat in my head and I've pulled him by the chain and got him over and wrapped it round his fuckin' froat. He's chokin'. I choked him till he passed out. Take our block? No fuckin' way.

They shout up the street.

VELVETBLADE Bunch of fuckin' wankers!

MR SMITH   We shat ya, ya fuckin' shitters.

SHRIMPDICK We done ya, ya big dumb

VELVETBLADE Bunch of fuckin' wankers!

MR SMITH   We shat ya, ya fuckin' shitters.

SHRIMPDICK We done ya, ya big dumb

GIRLY   Loser, toad's spunk

VELVETBLADE Rat face pig-arse fuckers

MR SMITH   We done ya!

SHRIMPDICK We done ya!

ALL   We done ya! *(A beat)*

GIRLY   This calls for a celebration.

They snort some speed. Velvetblade gets a knife out. Velvetblade passes the knife around.

VELVETBLADE Whatcha think, Girly?

GIRLY *(thoughtful, studies it.)* Beautiful.

VELVETBLADE Shrimpdick?

SHRIMPDICK Nice one, Velvetblade.

VELVETBLADE Mr Smith?

MR SMITH   That's class. Come in handy down football that would, Velvetblade.

VELVETBLADE Nah. This one's special. It's the weight. It's the crafting of the blade. It's the look of it. As Girly said. It's beautiful.

GIRLY   How many have you got now?

MR SMITH   Must be three hundred now.

VELVETBLADE Nah. Three hundred 'n twenty six.

MR SMITH   You spare a few?

VELVETBLADE Nah. Your mum'd never let you have 'em in the house, mummy's boy.

MR SMITH   Fuck off. She'd be alright. It's my Keeley I'd be worried about.

SHRIMPDICK   You ever moving in with her or what?

MR SMITH   I would but I'd miss me mum's cooking. That's the one thing I hated about being inside. I missed it. Me mum's grub. Keeley's idea of a classy meal is a baked bean omelette.

VELVETBLADE Who fuckin' eats that?

MR SMITH   My life. That's what she done for me the other night.

SHRIMPDICK   So you'll eat Keeley but not her grub?

MR SMITH   Yeah. Not that it's any of your business you nosy git. Least I got a bird, mate.

SHRIMPDICK   I do alright. I aint got one at the moment. Playing the field, son.

VELVETBLADE Yeah. I wonder why you aint got one?

MR SMITH   The clue's in the name. *(They laugh.)*

SHRIMPDICK   That was ten fuckin' years ago. One cold morning in the swimming pool, I get called Shrimpdick for ten years. Got used to it now. Had a complex about it. I'd go into a bar. "Oi! Shrimpdick!" Yeah? I'd go. "I'm huge" and I'd whip it out.

MR SMITH   To prove it, like?

SHRIMPDICK   Yeah, to prove it.

VELVETBLADE   Yeah.

SHRIMPDICK   So it all come on top. I've got that pissed off with it. I spent a year taking me dick out in public just to prove meself. Geezer in a bar says, "Oi! Why you called Shrimpdick?" I didn't think twice. I dropped me strides and whipped out me dong, yawning at the same time. Bored, sort of thing. Undercover copper, wasn't he? Nicked. Give me a tug, the bastard.

VELVETBLADE   Only tug you normally get is off yourself.

SHRIMPDICK   I get plenty mate.

Velvetblade's mobile phone rings.

VELVETBLADE   *(on phone)* Yeah. Yeah. Yeah. Yeah... I can't help it if he's crying. Can't you take him round your mum's house? She can babysit for a change... Yeah. Alright. Won't be long... Yeah. Yeah. I know, me dinner's in the dog. Love you too, angel... *(ends call)*

Mr Smith and Shrimpdick laugh.

VELVETBLADE   Alright, alright.

SHRIMPDICK   Yeah. It's really good having a bird, aint it?

MR SMITH   Yeah. And a kid.

VELVETBLADE   Always fuckin' moaning, she is. And the kid screaming all the time. It's designed. That sound. Designed by nature to do your head in.

GIRLY *(quietly)* It was the noise that evolved. Over centuries.
So a mother could find her baby in the long grasses or
trees or different terrain that our ancestors used to inhabit.

The lads look at each other.

VELVETBLADE Exactly. I was just getting on to that bit.

MR SMITH   Course you was.

VELVETBLADE Watch it you. Anyway. I'm better off out the
house.

MR SMITH   Talking a cocks. *(They look at him)*
I was in this posh bar up west with Keeley. Birthday treat.
She'd been going on about this place. Well famous. All the
celebrities go down there an' all that. So we've gone down
there an' I'm in the bog. You know. Smart one. Towels.
Marble. Designer cologne and after shaves. This little
attendant geezer sitting there in his uniform. So I'm at it.
Nice long piss. You know. That game you play of dive-
bombing them little antiseptic cubes in the urinal with your
jet stream. *(They all nod)* Then I hear this voice. "Wash
your cock, sir?" Sort of cheerful but business-like. I thought
I'd imagined it. Pissed and drugged up, yeah? So I went
back to me game. By now, I was doing a dambuster's
bombing run along the urinal. Then I hear it again. "Wash
your cock, sir?" I didn't look left or right. But it was the
attendant geezer in uniform. Fuck me, I thought. These
posh blokes even expect someone to do that for 'em.
"Wash your cock, sir?" The voice was slightly posh but still
London, if you know what I mean. Like you see on the
telly. Them things by – you know. Like with chimney
sweeps an' that.

GIRLY *(quiet, dreamy.)* Victorian England?

MR SMITH   Yeah. That's it. "Wash your cock, sir?" he goes
again. Well, I had to look round by then. He's standing
there with a towel draped over his arm and a smile on his
face. "Wash your cock, sir?"

GIRLY   You're telling us you were asked if you wanted your cock washed by a Victorian chimney sweep?

MR SMITH   Yeah. "Wash your cock, sir?" he goes, tugging his forelock.

VELVETBLADE People don't fucking tug their forelocks no more.

SHRIMPDICK What's a fucking forelock, anyway?

MR SMITH   I don't fuckin' know but he'd a tugged it if he'd 'ad one.

VELVETBLADE So what you do?

MR SMITH   I thought – this is too fucking weird and I goes to him "Do people do this all the time in here?" He goes "Oh no, sir. I only do it for my special customers. "*(beat)* I fuckin' legged it out of there.

They laugh. Pause. Girly has moved away from them, looking into the water.

SHRIMPDICK Girly alright?

VELVETBLADE Yeah. Just in one of his moods.

SHRIMPDICK See him at it?

MR SMITH   I never seen anyone get stuck in like that before. Is he fuckin' scared a' nothing or what?

VELVETBLADE Fuckin' fearless. I never seen no one fight like him. You know what he's like. Bit moody.

MR SMITH   Bit weird. You know. Books. Art galleries. What's all that about?

VELVETBLADE Do you any day.

MR SMITH   I know. I know. Just saying.

SHRIMPDICK When he leads the crew into a ruck – you know you're gonna be OK.

Ship's foghorn sounds. Mournful. They all stop. Listen.

GIRLY   Listen to that. Sound like the oldest whale in the world's great great grandfather.

MR SMITH   That's just what I was thinking.

Foghorn again

VELVETBLADE I know what it sounds like.

GIRLY   What? The Ghost of the River? The distressed souls of the spirits of the dead? The deep perturbed River God mourning for the dead of the world?

VELVETBLADE No. A ship's foghorn.

MR SMITH   No. Don't be stupid. He's talking different. What it sounds like.

GIRLY   Yeah. Good.

MR SMITH   What it sounds like in yer head.

GIRLY   Thassit.

VELVETBLADE What does it sound like then?

MR SMITH   I know what it sounds like.

GIRLY   What?

MR SMITH   It sounds like a great steaming plate of me mum's sausage and mash.

Velvetblade's mobile phone rings.

VELVETBLADE Yeah. Great. *(hands it to Girly)*

GIRLY   Yeah. *(ends call.)* Come on, it's kicked off down by the railway bridge. There's thirty of 'em.

MR SMITH   Thirty what? Who? Victorian Chimney Sweeps? What?

GIRLY   Yeah. We're gonna have a fight with thirty Victorian Chimney Sweeps. Like it.

SHRIMPDICK   Won't we get covered in soot?

VELVETBLADE 'kin 'ell.

GIRLY   It's them bastards from Elm Tree. Let's
fucking ave 'em.

They run off, chanting: 'Eden Crew! Eden Crew! Eden Crew!'

SCENE 3
Jeremy Wonfrey's Office.

JEREMY   So you've got La Scala on Wednesday, the
Albert Hall on Friday, the Met on Monday and then you'll be
with us again for rehearsals on Wednesday.

DEBORAH   Oh.

JEREMY   What?

DEBORAH   Just a shiver.

JEREMY   Cold?

DEBORAH   No. Hot. Hot and cold.

JEREMY   What?

DEBORAH   When you said all that I – I just wondered.
Wondered what you were talking about.

JEREMY   It's you darling. Better get used to it.

DEBORAH   Yeah. It's like being in the back of a very fast
luxury car. Exhilarating. Intoxicating. And totally powerless.
Not at the wheel. Oh, I don't know.

JEREMY   What is it darling?

DEBORAH   Do I seem comfortable?

JEREMY   Comfortable?

DEBORAH   Comfortable. Do I seem like I'm...

JEREMY   Is this – ?

DEBORAH   No. Well. Yes, I suppose it is.

JEREMY   Darling. This is just something that you'll get
more used to.

DEBORAH   You think so?

JEREMY   Yes. You're enjoying it aren't you?

DEBORAH   Oh yeah. Sometimes. When I'm singing. When I'm in the moment and nowhere else. I'm in heaven. There's been no past. There is no future. A golden globule of now. I'm where I should be. I'm doing what I came on to this earth to do.

JEREMY   So?

DEBORAH   I don't know. Last week. After a concert. I felt so – alone. Sitting in this ridiculous, posh hotel room on my own. Wondering how I got there.

JEREMY   Come on Debbie.

DEBORAH   Be honest, Jeremy.

JEREMY   No one gives a damn about all that.

DEBORAH   Long way.

JEREMY   What?

DEBORAH   Long way from Eden Housing Estate.

JEREMY   Sweet really.

DEBORAH   Thanks a lot.

JEREMY   Come on, darling I'm only joking. People love you. It takes a lot more guts and determination to achieve what you've achieved.

DEBORAH   I know, but...

JEREMY   Yes. That's why you're so popular with this... growing audience. You're a constant reminder that opera is for the people. Which it should be. You're a breath of fresh air. Most exciting thing to happen to the House since I've been running it.

DEBORAH   That's sweet, but it's more than...

Jeremy's phone rings.

JEREMY   Sorry. Jeremy Wonfrey. Yes of course. That's easy: To maintain the highest levels of excellence while constantly widening the appeal to a broader audience. To give access without lowering standards... Not at all...

(To Deborah) Sorry. That was the *Suddeutsche Zeitung*. Wanted a brief comment on my cultural vision for the House. 'My cultural vision for the House'. God Bless the Germans. In England the highest level of enquiry is usually "So how are you going to resolve your budget deficit?"

DEBORAH   Yeah.

JEREMY   So please don't worry. You're going to be fine.

DEBORAH   I'm not worried. It's just this feeling. I know how lucky I am. It's what I've always wanted, but it's more to do with – *(His phone rings)*

JEREMY   Sorry. Jeremy Wonfrey. Look Martin we can't let that designer back in this house. He totally ruined our *Ariadne* last year. *(beat)* No. The opera. Not the chorus member. Yes. Oh, Martin? Find an elegant way of putting that to his agent, will you? And a few calls to chums in Europe and the States. They'll appreciate the warning. Favours, Martin. Is that dinner with the Arts Council people still on? Yes. My club. Yes, they love it. The corner table by the window. Fine. Bye. *(To Deborah)* Sorry about that.

DEBORAH   That's OK.

JEREMY   Debbie...

DEBORAH   Look. It's OK. Another time.

JEREMY   Look, it's not as if you appear uncomfortable. You comport yourself with such dignity.

DEBORAH   I'm OK really. It's just... There's always this ... look in their eyes after performances.

JEREMY   Are you sure?

DEBORAH   Yes. But it's not just social or something. It's my soul.

JEREMY   What?

DEBORAH   My soul.

JEREMY   Oh come now. Please.

DEBORAH   Don't do that. Don't reduce what I'm feeling here. You can never know what it feels like. You're comfortable with them.

JEREMY   Come on, you're just feeling a bit down at the moment.

DEBORAH   Sure.

JEREMY   Priestess. You sing. The tribe hear ancestral voices. They don't disrespect you. They fear your power.

DEBORAH *(light)* Oh piss off!

JEREMY   Darling. Don't worry. Let's not argue. I'm merely positing a bit of pop-social anthropology.

DEBORAH   You posited something else just now.

JEREMY   You know what I mean. Don't be vulgar.

DEBORAH   But I am. I am vulgar. It's just behind the *Hermes* scarf. It's just under the haute couture veneer.

JEREMY   No – you're a creature of the most refined sensibilities. You are one of nature's princesses. Wherever you came from.

He kisses her.

DEBORAH   And your wife?

JEREMY   What about her?

DEBORAH   What about her sensibilities?

JEREMY   I don't want to talk about her.

DEBORAH   I feel so guilty.

JEREMY   I don't know why. We were separated.

DEBORAH   I know. Before we started our... whatever it is.

JEREMY   I don't want to talk about it now.

DEBORAH   And your kids?

JEREMY   Deborah, please.

DEBORAH   Oh, I'm Deborah now, am I? Not Debbie?

JEREMY   You know I don't like talking about her.

DEBORAH   Do you love them?

JEREMY   Please...

DEBORAH   Do you? Do you?

JEREMY   Of course I do.
DEBORAH   And me? Not that I care whether you do or not.
   I'm just curious.
JEREMY   You know I do.
DEBORAH   And my voice?
JEREMY   Yes. It's sublime.
DEBORAH   What if I didn't have it?
JEREMY   What?
DEBORAH   My voice. If I didn't have my voice? Would you
   still love me?
JEREMY   Darling...
DEBORAH   Would you?
JEREMY   That's purely academic.
DEBORAH   Would you?

Jeremy looks at her. Lights fade slowly.
Loud music plays as the lights come up on:

SCENE 4
The Estate. Night. The gang hang out.

SHRIMPDICK   One cold swimming pool. Ten years ago.
GIRLY   Enough. Button it, Shrimpdick.
VELVETBLADE   Here. I've got one. What's the difference
   between a pit-bull terrier with rabies and my girlfriend with
   PMT?
MR SMITH   What?
VELVETBLADE   Lipstick.

Mr Smith, Velvetblade and Shrimpdick laugh.

GIRLY   A spaceship. I sometimes wish a spaceship
   would land and take me off into another world. A world

without concrete. A world without bus stops. A world without you lot. Some sort of world where nothing is what you thought it was. All new. All of it fuckin' new... Velvetblade, you got any more speed?

VELVETBLADE Yeah. *(starts to prepare some of it)* Least this stuff is healthy. Healthiest thing I do. I look on it as me greens. I really gotta give up smokin' though.

SHRIMPDICK You go for that chest x-ray?

VELVETBLADE Yeah.

MR SMITH What they say?

VELVETBLADE Bit serious, as it goes.

MR SMITH Fuckin' 'ell mate, what you got?

VELVETBLADE The doctor looked at me dead serious and he goes, 'I'm sorry to have to tell you this Mr Velvetblade...'

MR SMITH Oh shit.

VELVETBLADE 'I'm, sorry to have to tell you this, but – well...'

SHRIMPDICK Come on. What'd he say?

VELVETBLADE 'I'm sorry to have to tell you this but – you've got an Albanian dwarf living in your lungs.'

MR SMITH *(believes it)* You ain't, have you?

VELVETBLADE Yeah. He showed me on the x-ray. You could see him. Little red hat. Beard. Little stove. Cooking his tea. Putting his feet up. Slippers. And the cheeky sod was smoking a fag.

MR SMITH Little sod. That's what give you the trouble, then. Can the Housing people get rid of him?

VELVETBLADE Yeah. They're trying to evict him next Tuesday.

MR SMITH Too right.

VELVETBLADE Yeah. I mean. Bloody liberty. I mean, you can't just let an Albanian dwarf live in your lungs willy nilly.

SHRIMPDICK No – 'cos then they all start to move in.

MR SMITH   Yeah. They tell their mates. Realise you're a soft touch.

VELVETBLADE   Before you know it, you've got a lung full of Albanian dwarves.

MR SMITH   Having all night parties.

SHRIMPDICK   I mean – how would you sleep?

MR SMITH   Them Albanians like to dance an' all.

SHRIMPDICK   Piss-taking little bastards. You could get onto the council to evict 'em but the social workers'll just say boo fuckin' hoo, they ain't got nowhere else.

MR SMITH   We should go down your lungs ourselves and give 'em all a good fucking kicking. *(opens Velvetblade's mouth, shouts)* Oi! You! Albanian! Get your little arse out me mate's lungs. You got one warning. You ain't gone by the morning, I'm coming down to get ya.

VELVETBLADE *(pushes him away.)* Fuck off.

MR SMITH   What's the matter? I'm only tryin' to help.

VELVETBLADE   I dunno. I got used to him in a way.

SHRIMPDICK   Sorta company, yeah?

VELVETBLADE   Yeah. Got quite fond of him.

GIRLY *(applauds, laughs)* Yeah. That's what I need. Some sort of spaceship. Get me outa here.

MR SMITH   Yeah. I know whatcha mean. See what I'm saying? You're doing head-talk again. Fog horns. Space ships. Whales. We ain't thick. We know what you mean, you know what I mean? Like your imagination. Imagination. Like, imagination, sort of thing.

GIRLY   Yeah. Thassit.

SHRIMPDICK   Yeah. Just 'cos you was the brainy one in school, don't mean we can't get ya, you know what I'm sayin'?

GIRLY   You know what I mean?

MR SMITH   Brainy but hard.

VELVETBLADE   Well hard.

MR SMITH   The hardest.

SHRIMPDICK   Oh yeah.

VELVETBLADE   Reckon he's the hardest on the estate.

MR SMITH   Yeah.

GIRLY   Do you mind?

MR SMITH   What?

GIRLY   Do you mind not talking about me in the third person?

SHRIMPDICK   But there's four of us.

GIRLY   Shut the fuck up. Give us some speed.

The gang snort the drugs.

MR SMITH   Yeah, Girly is the hardest. I can do Shrimpdick. Velvetblade can do me and Girly can do all of us.

GIRLY   Yeah. Just something. Something to happen.

An old blind man with a walking stick walks on. He is trying to get by with difficulty.

MR SMITH   Wanna hand, mate?

VELVETBLADE   You OK?

SHRIMPDICK   Need a bit of help, chum?

They go over to him. Girly watches.

OLD BLIND MAN   Thank you, boys.

MR SMITH   This should help you mate.

They take his arm, lead him. Girly watches.

SHRIMPDICK   We wanna help you, old-timer.

OLD BLIND MAN Thanks, lads.

VELVETBLADE   Try this, you old cunt. *(kicks his stick away)*

OLD BLIND MAN No don't, please.

MR SMITH   Fuckin' old wanker.

SHRIMPDICK   I hate blind old cunts like you.

They start pushing him from one to the other. Girly watches.

OLD BLIND MAN Please. Stop. In the name of God. Stop.
  (falls over)

VELVETBLADE   You fuckin' old tosser.

MR SMITH   Can't even stand up.

SHRIMPDICK   You're spoiling our fun, arse-face.

VELVETBLADE   Let's cut his dick off.

They begin to take the man's trousers down.

VELVETBLADE/SHRIMPDICK/MR SMITH *(venom)* Old!
  Old! Old! Old! Old! Old!

OLD BLIND MAN Please. Please. No.

SHRIMPDICK   Lop off his dick, Velvetblade.

*Velvetblade takes out a straight blade razor and moves
towards the old man's groin. Old Blind Man screams.*

MR SMITH *(holds his mouth)* Shut it, grandpa.

VELVETBLADE   Say goodbye to it, you old wanker. *(is about
  to use the razor)*

GIRLY   Stop it.

VELVETBLADE   What?

GIRLY   Let him go, Velvetblade.

VELVETBLADE   Piss off, Girly.

GIRLY   I'll fuckin' do the lot of you 'less you let him go.

They reluctantly release the old man. Girly goes over, helps him up.

GIRLY   Sorry, mate.

OLD BLIND MAN Thank you. Thank you. What have I done? Why? Why did they...?

GIRLY   No reason. They shit reasons.

OLD BLIND MAN *(panic)* Just a few of us. The bombing raid ended. We jumped over the side of the ship. It was on fire. Smell of petrol, aviation fluid, gasoline. The sea was on fire. My mate, Dave, on fire. His face. His face melted. I couldn't save him. Friends on fire. Screaming and drowning. The ship started to sink. Our home sinking. The Nazis came back, shooting at us in the water. I wanted to die. I wanted to go under. I needed to die and rest in the soothing wet flames. I didn't. I lived...

The bleak loneliness of "Wintereisse" by Schubert [Hurdy Gurdy] plays as we fade to black.

SCENE 5

Lights up on Jeremy's Office.

DEBORAH   Mistress. Strange word. Always hated it. Never thought I'd be one. When I was a kid, I always thought I'd marry and have kids and live in a nice council flat with a good husband. Mistress... Like those women on the telly. All they do is sit in posh apartments all day in silk night-gowns and their sole diet is champagne and chocolates. That's all. Nothing else. All perfumed farts and pekineses. Mistress... Sounds exotic. Sounded far away. Like bouquets, *Chanel,* first night cards. Not me, somehow. Someone else.

JEREMY   Come on...

DEBORAH   That's me now, isn't it? It's like my name. Deborah Mullins. Even that's not me any more. When I read it in the paper it's like it's someone else. Someone else's applause. Someone else's life. Someone else's husband.

JEREMY What *is* the matter with you today?

DEBORAH Mistress.

JEREMY Look, we've been through this -

DEBORAH Mistress.

JEREMY Why do we have to go through all of this again – why now?

DEBORAH See how you'd react.

JEREMY Why now?

DEBORAH Do I love you?

JEREMY Do you?

DEBORAH I don't want you to finally break up with her.

JEREMY Then how –?

DEBORAH Yes I do. I do then, OK? I just don't – didn't want to be this kind of...

JEREMY I know.

A knock on the door.

JEREMY That'll be him.

DEBORAH Who?

JEREMY Simon Rillings.

DEBORAH Shall I leave?

JEREMY No. You're his leading lady after all.

DEBORAH What do you think of the score? His new piece?

JEREMY New. Actually, I think there's a crisis with new work at the moment.

DEBORAH This coming from 'Mr Champion of New Music'?

JEREMY Yes, but, you know...

DEBORAH What?

JEREMY   I don't know. There's just a feeling in the
zeitgeist. A change. A move towards melody. Toward
narrative. We've come a long way since the laboratory
ethos of Darmstadt. All about the purity of sound and to
hell with bourgeois concepts like audience response. Of
course that radicalism had to happen and yes, I was a
champion of it. The Darmstadt musical revolution was the
equivalent of the sexual revolution in the sixties: If it
moves, pluck it. Or stroke it. Or beat it. And that was fine. A
radical rejection of what went before. But now we can
afford to reassess our relationships, our commitments. To
melody, for example. To be adult about the aesthetic of
melody. Of narrative. Of confrontation and violence in art
and its ultimate value.

DEBORAH   You're not on the radio now you know, Jeremy.

JEREMY   Let's just say there are some formal and
stylistic questions about his work.

DEBORAH   Yes, I see. Well actually, I really like his score.
It's amazing. So confident. Such a sure hand. Such power.
Is he actually here now?

Another knock.

JEREMY   Don't get me wrong. He's a very good young
composer. And he's becoming very trendy at the moment
with a hip, young following. It's good for the House to be
associated with him.

DEBORAH   Associated?

JEREMY   Well, you know.

DEBORAH   Oh.

JEREMY   The elitisim tag really is dreary, you know.
Always good to rebuff it.

DEBORAH   Especially as the annual grant is under review.

JEREMY   So young. And so cynical. I haven't actually
read the score that closely to be honest.

DEBORAH   Jeremy, that's awful.

JEREMY   Come on. I've been snowed under recently. Meetings, lobbying. It's bloody endless. So I skimmed through it and there's this really horrific torture scene. It's disgusting actually. It'll close the place down. I'd be out on my arse. He'll have to change it.

DEBORAH   I see.

JEREMY   What do you mean?

DEBORAH   I see.

JEREMY   Oh come on.

DEBORAH   Look, if you haven't read it properly, how can you know the context of the scene?

JEREMY   Look, I can tell...

DEBORAH   What if he doesn't agree?

JEREMY   He will. He might have a following but he's got a long way to go. If this goes on here it'll seal his reputation. He's not stupid. He knows that.

DEBORAH   I see.

A knock again.

JEREMY   Come in.

A young composer, Simon Rillings, comes in, holding his score. Nervous.

JEREMY   Hello Simon. Come in. You've met Deborah Mullins? Simon Rillings.

SIMON   Yes. Once before. Hello.

DEBORAH   Hello.

JEREMY   Well congratulations on the final act.

SIMON   Thank you.

JEREMY   It's really an extraordinary work.

SIMON   Really?

JEREMY   Yes. Extraordinary.

DEBORAH   Extraordinary.

JEREMY   Yes.

SIMON   Extra-

JEREMY   Ordinary, yes.

SIMON   Ordinary?

JEREMY   No, extra-

DEBORAH   Ordinary.

SIMON   Extraordinary?

JEREMY   Yes. It has a stark boldness of style and yet what I really liked about it was the way you never really alienate with it. There's a real desire to communicate. You do. You do want to communicate, don't you?

SIMON   Yes.

JEREMY   Good. We value that here. I think that's very important. Popular and serious. Tough yet accessible. In a deconstructed sense, of course.

SIMON   Thanks.

DEBORAH   I love the energy of it.

SIMON   Thanks.

DEBORAH   And it's really sexy, somehow.

SIMON   Right.

A beat. Jeremy watches.

SIMON   Miss Mullins... you... you...

DEBORAH   Call me Debbie.

SIMON   Yes. You... you lived on Eden Estate, didn't you?

DEBORAH   Yes. I used to.

SIMON   Well, that's where I live.

DEBORAH   Really. Which block?

SIMON	Valley House.
DEBORAH	Never. I lived in Glade House.
SIMON	Really? That's next to Valley.
DEBORAH	Yeah. God what's it like now?
SIMON	Same.
DEBORAH	Is the pub still going?
SIMON	No. Kept being vandalised. Shut it down.
DEBORAH	Not surprised. Roughest pub in the area.
SIMON	Yeah.
DEBORAH	What school you go to?

Jeremy notices her accent is slightly changing. He watches them connect.

SIMON   Eden.

DEBORAH   Me too. What, you went to the Academy after that?

SIMON   Yeah. Few years after you.

DEBORAH *(laughs)* Coupla scruffs, aren't we? Lowering the tone. Couple of Eden kids here, eh? Great.

SIMON   Yeah.

JEREMY   Perhaps you'll be the founders of a new movement. The Eden School of British composition. Has a ring to it. *(beat)*

DEBORAH *(to Simon)* So, well done you. You've written a bloody good piece, Simon. I can't wait to do it.

SIMON   I can't believe it.

DEBORAH   What?

SIMON   Like a dream. Deborah Mullins – wanting to do my work.

DEBORAH   Don't be such a silly sod, Simon. And I told you. Call me Debbie. And you'd better get used to compliments cos it's great what you've done.

SIMON   Thanks. I mean. Your voice – inspired me. It's written with your... colours and texture in mind.

DEBORAH   Did you get the piss taken out of you at Eden?

SIMON   Yeah.

DEBORAH   Not surprised. Me too. *(They laugh together)*

JEREMY   So. If we could just...

SIMON   Of course. Sorry Mr Wonfrey.

JEREMY   That's quite alright. As I said, the piece is remarkably good. Pungent. Earthy. Tough characters with plenty to say.

SIMON   Thank you.

JEREMY   But it needs a few changes.

SIMON   Really?

JEREMY   Oh yes.

SIMON   Right. Sure.

JEREMY *(opens score)* Here, for instance. Couldn't this motif come back more often?

SIMON   You want more of that theme?

JEREMY   Yes. Yes, I think so. That alright?

SIMON   Well...

JEREMY   Good.

SIMON   Right.

JEREMY *(flipping pages)* Oh yes. This scene here. The torture scene.

SIMON   Yes.

JEREMY   Is it necessary? What has he done to deserve it?

SIMON   It connects with what happens in the first scene.

JEREMY   Do you really think so? I wonder.

SIMON   Oh.

DEBORAH   Should I leave you to this?

JEREMY   No Debbie, please stay. You see I think it might just alienate people. In the wrong way. Communication. Important, yes? So lead them, Simon. Like you've done with melody. Lead them. Let them in.

SIMON   Yes. Well – I – I actually I – what I mean is... sorry I'm not making myself very clear but... well...

JEREMY   I just think you're capable of a bit more here, that's all. Reach, Simon. Reach beyond yourself. Don't shut them out. It's not me. I can understand the need to look unflinchingly at the darker side of human nature. But we have to think of our audience. Lead them. Let them in.

SIMON   So you want me to cut it?

JEREMY   Well certainly start to re-evaluate and rational-ise it on the way to probable excision, yes.

SIMON   Oh.

JEREMY   I'm afraid so. For the good of the piece, of course.

SIMON   Well , to be honest, I'd prefer not to.

JEREMY   I'm sorry?

SIMON   I'd prefer not to cut that because musically I've constructed it so that the torture is a kind of way he learns about himself. I personally hate violence or cruelty of any kind. With respect, sir, I'm sorry I live in a world where that... dark... needs to be shown. But I do.

JEREMY   Oh. Right.

SIMON   If that's OK?

JEREMY   Oh.

DEBORAH   Well – I'd better –

JEREMY   No. Debbie. You stay here please.

SIMON   I'd rather not cut it please. Not that section. Any other section in fact.

JEREMY   Oh. Oh I see. This is your first full-length opera and you know best, do you?

SIMON   No. Of course not, I just –

JEREMY   Well, well, young man. I think you may be making a slight mistake. I've worked in opera for long enough to know what works and what doesn't.

SIMON   Absolutely but –

JEREMY   My board would never allow such a brutal scene to be portrayed on this historic stage. I personally may not mind, but they – well they are rather fuddy duddy.

SIMON   I see your point, Mr Wonfrey. But that section is crucial really.

JEREMY   Think about it. We can discuss it later if you like.

SIMON   I see what you mean, I do. It's just that it's the most important scene in the piece and if that goes then my entire concept goes –

JEREMY   Just mull it over. See how it progresses.

SIMON   I don't mean to be rude Mr Wonfrey but I can't just leave it at that.

JEREMY   Steady, young man...

SIMON   Because I know now... I already know. Three years... working on it. I can't.

JEREMY   Oh.

SIMON *(close to tears)* I can't cut that scene.

JEREMY   Well then, we may have to reconsider our options.

SIMON   What?

JEREMY   Reconsider. Consider whether to proceed.

SIMON   You mean...?

JEREMY   Yes. I'm afraid so. Unless you cut that scene.

SIMON   But please...

JEREMY   That'll be all for now. Very nice of you to drop in.

SIMON   No, I need this... I've been working on it... so long... but I can't... I can't cut that scene... please...

DEBORAH   Jeremy, maybe he's got a point.

JEREMY   I'm sorry?

DEBORAH   I think the character needs to reach that point
of desperation otherwise it won't work. What happens to
him needs to be that brutal. Why don't you think it works?
Specifically?

Pause.

JEREMY   Well. Good. Thanks for that.

SIMON   Thank you, Miss Mullins.

JEREMY   Thanks for coming in Simon.

SIMON   Right. Sorry. Yes.

JEREMY   Let me know when you've changed your mind.
Trust me. As Auden used to say to Henze: 'Aunty Knows
Best'. You'll see.

SIMON   Thank you. Yes.

He nervously backs out.

JEREMY   I can't believe you just did that.

DEBORAH   How could you do that to him?

JEREMY   You contradicted me, Debbie. In front of that
little... That jumped-up...

DEBORAH   Don't be such a snob, Jeremy.

JEREMY   Snob? God – what an over-used word that is.
Snob. Snob. Snob. Snob. Snob. Snob. Snob. If being a snob
means having a developed set of aesthetic and cultural
principles – what's so wrong about being a snob? Snob.
Snob. Good word, actually. Like the taste of it. Look, we're
in a difficult situation. Opera gets a bloody bad press.
Fuddy duddy. Outmoded. Government rapping our knuckles
for it. We have to get people like him involved to show
that... ordinary... well... that people like him are involved.
I don't dislike him personally. I'm sure he's terribly talented

but we have to maintain a balance. A lot of my board are against him working here. In this house. I've championed him against a lot of opposition. He came to a dinner recently. The old cliché: He actually didn't know which knife and fork to use. He smoked between courses. I had to light up too to spare his blushes. He's actually rather a nice chap. But he must remember – there are parameters. He can't just ride roughshod over the people who work here. Seasoned, professional experienced people. He must realise that there are ways of doing things. I've stuck my neck out for him.

DEBORAH   So you've commissioned him to keep the Government happy? Make it look like you've gone all populist, to get the cash.

JEREMY   I wouldn't put it quite as infelicitously as that.

DEBORAH   Bollocks. You *are* a snob.

JEREMY   It's only fair to let him know where he stands.

DEBORAH   To know his place, you mean.

JEREMY   He's out of his depth. I've helped him.

DEBORAH   I was out of my depth too. When I first met you. Are you helping him like you helped me?

JEREMY   I'm just being realistic. It can't go on with that scene.

DEBORAH   But you haven't even read the whole piece. He's right – it does connect with what happens in the first scene.

JEREMY   He could at least have met me half way. He's got to play the game just a little bit.

DEBORAH   Game? Is that what this is? He's from Eden Estate. He hasn't learnt to play the game yet. Thank God. Unlike – This piece is his life. You can see it. And you just walked all over it.

JEREMY   Debbie...*(He goes to touch her)*

DEBORAH *(pulls away)* Don't. You're screwing the pair of us, aren't you?

JEREMY   Debbie, come on...

DEBORAH   Don't. I've just seen – realised how you –

She looks at him, leaves. Jeremy sits on his own.

JEREMY   Snob.

Lights fade. Music: "Family Affair" by Sly & The Family Stone fades up with lights:

SCENE 6
Old Blind Man's flat. Girly helps the old man.

GIRLY   In you come, mate.

OLD BLIND MAN   Thank you.

GIRLY   Sit yourself down.

OLD BLIND MAN   Yes. Thank you. Oooh, my legs.

GIRLY   Did they do that?

OLD BLIND MAN   No. It's my arthritis. Got it in my legs. And my back. And my arms. And my fingers. And my feet. And my toes. I'm surprised I haven't got it in my hair too.

GIRLY   You gonna be OK now?

OLD BLIND MAN   Yes. Thanks for what you did.

GIRLY   'S OK. Well – I'll be off then.

OLD BLIND MAN   Would you mind staying for a bit?

GIRLY   Well...

OLD BLIND MAN   Please. Just for a little while. Nice to chat.

GIRLY   'Spose.

OLD BLIND MAN   Thank you... Why? Why did they do that to me?

GIRLY   I dunno.

OLD BLIND MAN   No respect. I know the old folks always think the younger generation isn't up to much. Our parents thought the same as us – so did theirs. And theirs. But now. Now it's different. It is. The soul's gone. Some... dead soul, some great big dead soul's sitting on this country. No values. No love. Junk food. Junk minds. Junk hearts. Sorry.

GIRLY   'S alright.

OLD BLIND MAN   Poor. That's what we are now. Impoverished.

GIRLY   How long have you lived here?

OLD BLIND MAN   Too long. This bloody estate. When the wife passed away this was the only place I could get. Had to move out of me old place. Couldn't cope on me own.

GIRLY   Got any family?

OLD BLIND MAN   Got a son. Well, he's my grandson, really. But me and my wife looked after him after his mum passed on. When he was quite small. He is my son, really. Calls me Dad. Just me and him now... Good Lad. He wouldn't do what they did. I brought him up with love. Encouragement. Doing quite well for himself.

GIRLY   Listen, I'd better be going...

OLD BLIND MAN   Smells of decay, this place. Feel the crunch of broken glass and the slide of take-away food wrappers under my feet. Dog dirt. Foul language. Curses. Smell of fear. Greed. See – I live in a dark world. A dark world of fear and pain. Constant pain in the darkness. But I can still feel the sun on my face. When I go for a walk in the park, I can smell the grass. And I can hear small children playing. I hear the odd kind remark. And that gives me hope. I can still feel the rain on my face and hands. I can smell the bread from the bakery. And that makes me want to live. Sometimes. Sometimes I want to live. And there's music. There's always music... Press that tape button, would you? Please? *(Girly does so. We hear Schubert's Quintet in C Minor, Slow Movement.)* God, doesn't that sound like... like... heaven?

GIRLY 'S alright. Yeah.

OLD BLIND MAN I always loved music. Good music. Encouraged my son to listen to this sort of music. The music that lifts up your soul. That shares your sadness. It keeps me alive. Music.

GIRLY How'd you go blind?

OLD BLIND MAN During the war.

GIRLY What you said before?

OLD BLIND MAN Yes. Our ship was bombed by the Nazis.

They listen in silence to the music. The old man gets up, starts to dance slowly to the music. He stops, starts to cry. Girly goes over to him, puts hand on his shoulder. The old man touches it. He makes his way over to the tape machine, feels for another tape, puts it on. Thirties song, "The Sun Has Got His Hat On" plays. Bright. Insanely optimistic. He starts to dance to it. He grabs Girly, dances with him. Girly is embarrassed but goes along with it. A man comes in. It is Simon, the young composer. He is carrying the score from the meeting.

SIMON Dad? What you doin'? Dad?

OLD BLIND MAN Simon, is that you?

SIMON Yes Dad. Who's this?

RILLINGS Oh. This young man helped me. I was being attacked.

SIMON *(shock)* You OK, Dad? *(goes over to him)*

RILLINGS Oh yes. Thanks to this young man.

SIMON Oh. Thanks. *(shakes Girly's hand)*

GIRLY No problem. I better go now then.

RILLINGS Just a minute, young man. I've got something for you. How did your meeting go, Simon?

SIMON You sure you're OK?

RILLINGS Yes.

SIMON Did you call the police?

GIRLY   Didn't have to. I sorted it.

SIMON   Are you sure?

GIRLY   Yeah. He's OK now.

SIMON   You weren't hurt, were you?

RILLINGS   No, no. Bit shaken up but I'm fine.

SIMON   Oh god.

RILLINGS   I'm fine, Simon. Don't worry.

SIMON   Yeah, but if I'd been there...

RILLINGS   I'm fine now. What about your meeting? *(proudly, to Girly)* My son's a composer, you know. He makes music. He's written an opera.

SIMON   Dad, he doesn't want to know about –

RILLINGS   He'll be on the radio soon. 'Midweek Arts Roundup'. It's the best. And he'll be on it.

GIRLY   Oh.

RILLINGS   So how was your meeting?

SIMON   It was a disaster, Dad. Jeremy Wonfrey wants me to cut the most important scene.

RILLINGS   But why? What reason did he give?

SIMON   I didn't really understand what he was saying, talks in this way you can't understand.

RILLINGS   You didn't lose your temper, did you Simon?

SIMON   Well...

RILLINGS   Did you?

SIMON   No, but...

RILLINGS   Good – you must keep these sort of people happy. Humour him. Accept his ideas if you can.

SIMON   But I can't, Dad. If I let it go on without that scene, I'll be lying to myself.

RILLINGS   Was it just him at the meeting?

SIMON   No, actually. Deborah Mullins was there.

RILLINGS   Deborah Mullins? She's wonderful. Is she still down to play the lead role?

SIMON   Yeah...

RILLINGS   That's marvellous.

SIMON   She stuck up for me.

RILLINGS   Good. Maybe he'll change his mind then.

SIMON   No. I doubt it somehow. He's never liked me. He can smell this place on my skin.

RILLINGS   Nothing to be ashamed of. Are you ashamed, young man?

GIRLY   Well...

RILLINGS   You are who you are. You've written a great opera and it's going on.

SIMON   Dad, I can't let it go on without that scene. Why the hell did I get involved with all this? This fuckin' posh music world. I should have stayed playing jazz. Or rock music. I'm sick of the snobbery. I'm sick of the right smiles, the right codes. I'm sick of it all, Dad. *(throws the score on the floor)*

RILLINGS *(hugs him)* Simon, my boy. My son. I love you. I know you're frustrated but you must go on. It's your duty. It's your duty to your God-given talent. You mustn't let the small cripple you. You must go on. Don't drown. Go on.

SIMON   I can't, Dad. Maybe I don't want to.

RILLINGS   You must. You're Simon Rillings, remember. Your work will still be here, God willing, when the Jeremy Wonfreys of this world are dead and buried. Buried with all their petty jealousies, their fears, their prejudices. Because he is jealous, son. For all his wealth, for all his position, he cannot create.

SIMON   But he doesn't have to, Dad. He's better off that way.

RILLINGS   Then pity him. Pity his jealousy and continue. Beethoven – look at what suffering that man endured. He lost one of his faculties. The most important for a composer and he lived – and he triumphed and God blesses us with his genius to this day. You must, Simon. You must.

SIMON   OK, OK, Dad. But it's not that easy. Not for me. Way you talk. It doesn't work like that any more, Dad.

RILLINGS   What do you think, young man?

GIRLY   This geezer your boss? This Jeremy geezer?

SIMON   Yeah.

GIRLY   Then your Dad's right, mate. Keep him sweet. Then do what you want.

SIMON   Cheers.

GIRLY   What's all that about then?

SIMON   What?

GIRLY   The composing. You know. What, do you...

SIMON   What?

GIRLY   You like, write the actual music? The dots?

SIMON   Yeah. Exactly. The dots.

GIRLY   Don't get many of you lot round here. Didn't know people still did it.

SIMON   Yeah.

GIRLY   Make a living at it?

SIMON   Just about.

GIRLY   Nice one. I'd like to do that. I like music.

SIMON   Yeah. Why don't you then?

GIRLY   Nah.

SIMON   Why not?

GIRLY   Well... you know.

SIMON   Yeah. I do actually.

GIRLY   Yeah. Let him hear what he wants to hear. Then go for it. What you want. And do it for us.

SIMON   Us?

GIRLY   Yeah. The Eden Estate crew.

SIMON   Yeah.

GIRLY   Look, I better go now.

RILLINGS   You did a good thing today, young man.

SIMON   Yeah. Thanks for that, mate.

GIRLY   S' nothing. See ya.

RILLINGS   Oh yes. I want you to have this. *(gives him a tape)* Thank you.

GIRLY   Thanks. Bye.

He leaves.

SIMON   Dad, I couldn't say this in front of him...

RILLINGS   What, Simon?

SIMON   You. I love you. But you're different. It's not that simple. You didn't drown. Your mate...

RILLINGS   What about him?

SIMON   He went under.

RILLINGS   Yes.

SIMON   Well, maybe I'm more like him.

RILLINGS   Simon.

SIMON   Well, maybe I am, Dad. You could forgive. You're stronger than I am.

RILLINGS   You can't let a man like him drag you down.

SIMON   It's taken me three years to write that work. And he's decided to cut the most important section. Look, maybe I should just face up to it. I'm not cut out for this.

RILLINGS   You've got to keep going.

SIMON   Yeah. I'm the one who has to keep going. Not you.

RILLINGS   Simon..

SIMON   That's enough, OK. I'm sick of your bloody... relentless optimism. Just stop it OK. I don't have your strength. Your guts. I'm fucking weak, OK. Just shut up about fighting on. About surviving. Maybe I don't fuckng want to. Maybe I just can't take this any more.

Pause

RILLINGS   Well, if that's how you feel. If you want to just give up. Just like that.

SIMON   But it's not just like that. It's been years, Dad. Years of trying. Years of battling.

RILLINGS   But you're starting to do really well. You're getting a real following now.

SIMON   Yes but I'm really tired of it somehow, it doesn't seem to matter so much to me any more.

RILLINGS   It does to me, Simon.

SIMON   Exactly.

RILLINGS   What do you mean by that?

SIMON   Nothing.

RILLINGS   You're saying I pressurised you?

SIMON   No. No.

RILLINGS   Well, OK. All those years of sacrifice. Struggle for a dream. Letting it go. You really want to do that?

SIMON   No. Of course I don't want to. *(pause)* I've been meaning to say this for a while, Dad. You're the best person I've ever known.

RILLINGS   Are you – is everything alright, Simon?

SIMON   You – you've always been my...

RILLINGS   Simon...

SIMON   My inspiration, Dad. All the concerts you took me to as a kid. Having to get the last bus home and then walking back through the estate at night. Scary. But you were there. Felt safe with you. Saving up all your pennies for the tickets for all that amazing stuff. Plays. Music. Concerts. No one else did that round here. That's when people thought I was a bit weird. That's how it started.

RILLINGS   Don't think about that.

SIMON   No. I don't. That's not what I'm saying. I'm saying, "Thanks." Thank you. Thank you for caring enough to give me all that. It was worth standing out a bit.

Being a bit weird, whatever. The bands, the orchestras, the music. And you supported my dream, always.

RILLINGS   Simon... Simon...

SIMON   Where did it all come from? In you I mean?

RILLINGS   I don't know. I never had it as a kid. It just felt right, I suppose.

SIMON   I'm frightened, Dad.

RILLINGS   Why, Simon?

SIMON   Dad. You're getting older.

RILLINGS   Don't you worry about me.

SIMON   Dad, you're all I've got. I'm frightened of losing you. Frightened that someone'll break in and hurt you. Frightened that someone'll mug you in the street. Like what just happened to you. God, Dad you gotta be more careful.

RILLINGS   I'm alright son.

SIMON   But you're not, though, are you? You're always falling over. I'm always frightened every time the phone rings in case something's happened to you. You never remember to wear your alarm button. You're always refusing to let me help you.

RILLINGS   I'm set in my ways, Simon.

SIMON   You wouldn't even allow me to organise the shoppers to shop for you. Or to allow carers from the council in to help me to help you. God Dad I don't know how much I can bloody take. You're so difficult to help. I'm worried about you all the time, you won't even discuss going into a home.

RILLINGS   No, Simon. Not that.

SIMON   No. I know. I know. Don't worry. But in a way it's bloody selfish of you. Dad, I really can't cope any more. I've had enough of all of it. *(Rillings puts his hand on his son's shoulder. Simon touches it.)*

SIMON   Sorry Dad. I didn't mean...

RILLINGS   That's alright son. That's alright.

SIMON   Shit. Now I'm gonna hate myself for talking to you like that. Like I've wiped out all the good I've done for you. Sorry.

RILLINGS   Simon. Don't be so hard on yourself. You can never wipe out the good.

SIMON   You come from a different time, Dad. Not a perfect time. But a better time. Decency, honour, responsibility meant something. Well, now that's all gone. Even saying those words sounds yucky and weird. Why is that? And when you've gone. I'll be... I'll be all one me own in this kinda cruel new outer space of greed and fear. You're the last of a breed, Dad.

RILLINGS   I'll always be with you, Simon. And you. Those words you just mentioned. They're still here. You've got all those things in you.

SIMON   Yeah?

RILLINGS   Yeah. Course. Course you have.

SIMON   Come 'ere you.

He gets up and gives his dad a hug. They hold each other, swaying. Lights fade on them.

SCENE 7

Spotlight on Jeremy.

JEREMY *(on 'phone)* Yes, darling. How are the kids...? Good. ...Yes, I'll be away all weekend. Directors' conference in Zurich... Yes, yes, I'll miss you too. Got a few problems with the new piece... Yes. Shame really. Rillings... Yes – you know the type. Very chippy. Yes. Debbie Mullins is contracted for the *hauptrolle* ... Yes, yes, she's marvellous. Reminds me of your voice when you were still singing... Yes. No, you were. ...OK. Better dash, darling. Bye.

SCENE 8

Eden Housing Estate. Street. Night.
Loud music. The Gang run in. Elated.

SHRIMPDICK I don't believe it!

MR SMITH We done 'em again!

VELVETBLADE We never fuckin' lose!

TOGETHER Eden Crew! Eden Crew! Eden Crew!

GIRLY If we aint careful we'll be getting a bit of a reputation.

SHRIMPDICK Top Boys of the Top Crew.

MR SMITH They'll be coming from all over. We'll be well fuckin' famous.

SHRIMPDICK I think I'd be well suited to a life of celebrity. Temperentally, I mean.

MR SMITH Why's that then, Shrimpdick? *(pause)*

SHRIMPDICK *(thinks)* I dunno.

MR SMITH Oh.

VELVETBLADE I never seen anyone scared like that. That geezer you done, Girly.

GIRLY You were pretty useful yourself, mate. You were all fuckin' superb.

MR SMITH/SHRIMPDICK Ta Girly. Cheers mate.

GIRLY Way you worked that blade, though. Quality.

VELVETBLADE Ta mate, yeah. It's me special one.

GIRLY Tasty.

VELVETBLADE Yeah. S'funny. But I love all of em. My collection. Like if we've been having a row. Me an' her. Or the baby's crying. I just go in the lounge. At night. And look at me knife collection. Blinking in the street lights outside. Makes me feel all... lovely. All sorta sentimental. Yeah. I wonder how many people they've done in their time. All with their own stories.

GIRLY History?

VELVETBLADE Yeah.

GIRLY I was fuckin' prouda ya. Out there. I fuckin' love ya, ya bunch of Dozy Fuckers. *(beat. A moment between them.)*

TOGETHER Eden Crew! Eden Crew! Eden Crew!

Blackout.

SCENE 9

Jeremy's office. Jeremy and Deborah having sex on his desk. She is fully dressed apart from her underwear. He has his trousers off.'

JEREMY But Alban Berg is a genius. *Wozzeck* is one of the greatest modern works. Where are they now? Where are the Alban Bergs of today? Oh oh oh. Nowhere. That's where. Oooh... ooh... ooh...

DEBORAH It all depends where you're... aah, where you're ...oooh, where you're looking. You have to dig deeper... aah.

JEREMY Push hard till we find them.

DEBORAH You've got to be brave. Thrust your policies on new work even harder to the board.

JEREMY That board. They're so aah so stuck up. So aah rigid in their oh oh...

DEBORAH So... ah... uptight in their narrow conception.

JEREMY *(stops)* You have been careful, haven't you darling?

DEBORAH Yes. I know how that word frightens you. Oooh.

JEREMY *(continues)* I've got to keep prodding at them.

DEBORAH To make them come round.

JEREMY Push harder, prod harder to make them come... *(about to climax)*

DEBORAH To make them come... *(She suddenly stops)* I can't.

JEREMY What? What is it?

DEBORAH I just can't. Something's... I just can't OK?

JEREMY What?

DEBORAH I don't know.

A knock on the door.

JEREMY Shit.

SIMON *(off-stage)* Simon Rillings for Mr Wonfrey.

JEREMY Oh shit. Our meeting. I forgot.

DEBORAH You'd better let him in.

JEREMY I don't want to see him. Not now.

Knock on the door again.

DEBORAH *(mischievous)* Hide. *(She readjusts her skirt)*

JEREMY What?!

DEBORAH Hide under the desk.

JEREMY I'm not bloody well hiding –

DEBORAH I'll let him in now then. *(She goes to door)*

JEREMY Look – stop it. It's not funny. *(tries to get his trousers on but there's not enough time)* Debbie!

As the "door opens", he gets under desk.

DEBORAH Hello, Simon.

SIMON Hello, Miss Mullins. *(enters)* Is Mr Wonfrey here?

DEBORAH Not just at the moment.

SIMON Oh well...

DEBORAH   How's the re-writing going?

SIMON   Well... not very... well. I haven't...

DEBORAH   I think what you've done is wonderful, by the way. Even the so-called difficult scene.

SIMON   Thanks. Really?

DEBORAH   Yes. I don't think you should change a note.

SIMON   But Mr Wonfrey said...

DEBORAH   He'll come round. Eventually.

Jeremy bangs his head under the desk. Deborah hits it again to cover up, as if emphasising her point.

DEBORAH   Yes. He'll come round. He just has to keep the board happy.

SIMON   Are you sure?

DEBORAH   Yes. He's just a bit grumpy at the moment. Trouble at home.

JEREMY *(from under desk)* Right!

SIMON   What?

DEBORAH   I said "Right".

SIMON   But you didn't move your –

DEBORAH   My lips? I know. It's a new vocal technique I'm trying.

SIMON   Your voice...

DEBORAH *(adopts deeper voice)* Yes. It's a bit hoarse at the moment. A bit gruff.

JEREMY *(under desk)* A bit gruff?

SIMON   Yes. I heard you the first time. That's an amazing trick. The lips-not-moving thing.

DEBORAH   Seriously. You should just be confident and very pleased with what you've done. I'm really looking forward to singing it. There's some very tricky melisma in parts but I think I can manage it.

JEREMY *(under desk)* Do you now?

SIMON   What?

DEBORAH   Do you? Now? Do you think I can?

SIMON   Yes. Yes, of course.

JEREMY *(under desk)* Well, I don't.

SIMON   What?

DEBORAH   Well, I don't know every note yet but I'm sure I'll learn it.

SIMON   That's an amazing technique. How do you do it? I'd like to maybe incorporate it in the piece. Are you sure you like it?

DEBORAH   Yes. It's great.

SIMON   Thanks.

JEREMY *(under desk)* Rubbish.

SIMON   What?

DEBORAH   It's great.

SIMON   And you think it's got a chance of going on?

DEBORAH   Every chance.

SIMON   Thanks, 'cos I just recorded an interview about it on the radio.

DEBORAH   What programme?

SIMON   "Midweek Arts Roundup".

DEBORAH   Really? That's quite an accolade.

SIMON   Thanks.

JEREMY *(under desk)* You slut.

SIMON   Sorry?

DEBORAH   What?

SIMON   You just called me a slut.

DEBORAH   No. It's a term of endearment from me.

SIMON   Oh. Thanks.

JEREMY *(under desk)* Bitch.

SIMON   Another term of endearment?

DEBORAH   Yeah.

JEREMY *(under desk)* Stop this you little minx.

SIMON   Look, I can take a joke but...

JEREMY *(under desk)* Get out of here, you little runt.

SIMON   There's no need to talk to me like that.

Jeremy rises above the desk in his underpants.

JEREMY   If you think I'm going to continue this pathetic bedroom-farce for one more moment, you are mistaken.

SIMON   Mr Wonfrey!

DEBORAH   Yes – he'd just come back from the shower when you knocked.

JEREMY   Yes. The shower.

SIMON   I see.

JEREMY   No Simon, you do not *see*. Not in the sense that you say you see. You see?

SIMON   I see. I mean – right.

JEREMY   The shower. No time to change. Now. What do you want? *(He puts on his trousers)*

SIMON   I've decided to keep the scene as it is, Mr Wonfrey.

JEREMY   Have you now?

SIMON   Yes. Of course I'm prepared to discuss it fully with you but essentially it should remain the same.

JEREMY   Well I'm afraid that's it then. I'll tell the board of your decision.

SIMON   But Mr Wonfrey...

JEREMY *(snaps)* How dare you come in here and lay down your demands.

SIMON *(conciliatory)* They're not demands, Mr Wonfrey, they're just – I need to explain to you respectfully but clearly, why I can't fundamentally change the scene.

JEREMY *(white with rage)* Well let me respectfully but clearly explain to you that you are no longer writing a piece for this house. Or any other house for that matter.

DEBORAH Jeremy, for God's sake –

JEREMY Shut up. I'm attending a forum in Zurich at the weekend with the directors of all the major opera houses of Europe and I shall make it abundantly clear that you are difficult, Mr Rillings. Difficult. You do know what that means, don't you? Difficult? Diff-i-cult. Difficult. Difficult, difficult, difficult. Difficult.

DEBORAH Jeremy – stop. What are you doing?

JEREMY You'll be lucky if you can get a commission to write jingles for choccy bars on TV.

SIMON Please, Mr Wonfrey.

JEREMY Get out of here, Mr Difficult.

SIMON Difficult?

JEREMY Mr Rillings...

SIMON Look. I've been trying. Honest. I have... I've been trying to make it work without that scene and it doesn't. I promise you I've tried but I just can't seem to... it doesn't seem to be...

JEREMY Well? Look, if you can't even explain what you mean...

SIMON Can't. ...it doesn't... all of it hangs together with that scene... it musically and scenically depends on it.

JEREMY Right. Goodbye. Out you go then.

DEBORAH Jeremy!

SIMON OK. OK then. If you're not prepared to even discuss it then OK.

JEREMY That's right. Goodbye.

SIMON *(snaps)* Shut it, you. You know nothing. You know fuck-all about what it means to go into that lonely room. The lonely room of the heart. Where your mates from Eden Housing Estate despise you 'cos you're weird and you write

music. 'Cos you want to listen to angels singing in your
head instead of beating someone up? Well, Mr Wonfrey,
I haven't been beaten up and spat in the face for years to
be told I can't do it by someone like you. I aint gonna sell
out. Not me. You aint corrupting me. I know why you hate
me. How dare someone like me make music? How dare it
be good?

JEREMY   You have a rather high opinion of yourself. Now
get out.

SIMON   I've had to. I've had to have a high opinion of
myself. To live. To survive. But deep down. Deep down at
night. On my own. I'm full of fear. I wish I could fit in on
Eden Estate. But I know I can't. I'd be spat on just the
same. Like I'm spat on here. But at least here I can make
music. I'm covered in your spit. I'm dripping with it. But at
least I can make music. And you, Deborah Mullins. You're
wonderful. You're good. I can tell. You can sing my songs. I
trust you. Something... something about you... You're an
artist. Please. Sing my songs, Deborah Mullins. *(gives her
the score)*

JEREMY   Get out.

SIMON *(almost in a mystic trance, he looks at Jeremy)* I
curse you. I curse you and everyone like you. That smiling-
and-diary-schedule-meeting-in-perfumed-cushioned-offices-
drink-my-blood-and-murder-me. Me and all of us. You push
the buttons: we die. You write a letter: we don't eat. You
cut me down: my father cries. Because you can't create.
Like the devil. Only God creates. You destroy everything
you touch because you can't love. *You can't love. You can't
love. You can't love. You can't love.*

JEREMY   Get out of here!

SIMON *(screaming)* You can't love. You can't love. But I can.
I can even learn to love you. *Love you. Love you. Love
even you. I love you.*

JEREMY *(gets on 'phone)* Hello. Security? Send someone up
   to my office immediately.

SIMON   *I love you. I love you. I love you.*

Deborah is shocked, frightened, concerned.

SIMON   And the power of my love for you will live on.
   Live on in music. *I love you,* Mr Wonfrey.

*He kisses Jeremy. Jeremy pushes him away. Simon throws his
arms round Jeremy's neck, half strangling/half hugging him on
his desk.*

SIMON   I love you. I love you. I love you.

A Security Guard comes in. Gets Simon in a head-lock.

SIMON *(quieter)* I love you.

JEREMY   Get this – this – Get this out of my office.

SIMON   I love you all.

*Simon is roughly bundled out. Jeremy and Deborah look at
each other. Pause.*

DEBORAH   Oh my God, Jeremy. What have you done to
   him?

JEREMY   What do you mean? He attacked me.

DEBORAH   He was defending himself.

JEREMY   He's a bloody madman.

DEBORAH   Have you got any idea how he must be feeling
   now?

JEREMY   So what?

DEBORAH   This isn't about whether that scene's right or wrong. This is about you being right. About you being in control.

JEREMY   Don't give me that. Not now.

DEBORAH   What are you really?

JEREMY   That's enough.

DEBORAH   A bully? A school bully. Taking your private school pecking order into the workplace. Know your place isn't just a phrase for you, is it? It's a moral code. Follow the house rules or you get a thrashing in the house master's office. Is that what this is all about?

JEREMY   Oh, what a piercing insight.

DEBORAH   You really don't give a damn do you? You've just destroyed someone.

JEREMY   He destroyed himself.

DEBORAH   But he doesn't count does he? Like me when I started out.

JEREMY   You think you're there now, do you? You think you're – invulnerable?

DEBORAH   What do you mean?

JEREMY   It's about time you realised where you fit into all this. Look, it's all very well to preach that you're making a new audience for opera. To them. To the public. Salving the conscience of the Lord Turlington and his chums. If only they could just be honest about the joys of elitism. But they can't. They need you. The magical diva with the common touch. The opera star with the heart of the people. But this is me you're talking to. Me. Remember. Me. Me. Remember?

DEBORAH   I despise your lot. Yes – your lot. You and your gang. I know how I'd be treated if I didn't have this gift.

JEREMY   Your throat?

DEBORAH   My voice. I'd be ignored. Put back on the dump they say I came from. But oh no. I played the game. I was a good girl. Your people. They can buy everything. Helicopters. Hotels. Chateaux in the South of. France. The best wines. But the one thing you can't buy is talent. You hate that. You can't buy for yourselves what's already free. A Gift of God. And I can see the anger in your eyes that it's been given to someone who isn't one of yours. And because you can't buy the gift, you buy the people who have it. That's what Lord Turlington does. He bought me. That's me. Bought and bloody sold.

JEREMY   Rubbish. Simplistic, inaccurate rubbish.

DEBORAH   And maybe Simon's right. Be brave. Don't compromise. Don't be bought.

JEREMY   And don't work. Very bloody clever.

DEBORAH   I want you to re-open his commission.

JEREMY   What?

DEBORAH   Come with me now. You must find him and talk to him.

JEREMY   Are you serious?

DEBORAH   Yes. He's so hurt. So honest about what he's written. That's the most... real or passionate thing I've seen since I've been working here. I remember feeling like that. Once. You must talk to him, Jeremy. Give him another chance.

JEREMY   No. It would be highly inappropriate. Now stop this. You're going a bit too far this time.

DEBORAH   What did you mean about me not being invulnerable?

JEREMY   Well, I'm sure you will be my dear. One day.

DEBORAH   What are you saying? Are you threatening me?

JEREMY   We all need friends. Wherever we are.

DEBORAH   You can't bully me like you've bullied him. Yeah. You could damage me once but I'm safe now. And you know it.

JEREMY   Good for you.

DEBORAH   Right. I'm contracted to play the lead role in
    Simon's piece and if you don't do it I'll walk.
JEREMY   What?
DEBORAH   I'll walk from every other role in the season.
    Because of your breach of contract.
JEREMY   You wouldn't.
DEBORAH   Try me. *(beat.)*

Stand off. They stare at each other.
Lights cross fade.

SCENE 10

GIRLY *(on the street, thinking aloud)*
    I went to the museum the other day. Well, s' free aint it.
    Aint got fuck all else to do of a day. Went in. Saw this
    fantastic fuckin' statue. Warrior. In marble. Fuckin' massive.
    Big strong head. Eyes full of light and guts for the fight
    in front of him. "Alaric the Visigoth" he was called. Knocking
    on the gates of Rome. "Open up you corrupt fuckers your
    time is up". Like God's kissed the marble and melted it and
    twisted it round and put it there. Only he used an artist to
    do it. A human. Wish I could 'ave. Wish I could fuckin'
    make somefin'. Somefin' like that. Felt a bit sad. Then these
    tourists come in. Cameras. Didn't even look at the warrior.
    Just hid behind their cameras. Shielding 'emselves from the
    beauty. Like if they looked at it with the naked eye they'd
    be frozen and splintered. Or they'd have to fuckin' change.
    Change their fuckin' heads. So they hide behind their
    cameras. Scared of beauty. And what it might do to
    them. I wanted to scream at 'em. I wanted to take
    their cameras, smash em and scream "Look! Use your
    fuckin eyes, look! Don't be fuckin frightened. Look at this
    warrior and his honest bleedin' soul." But what good would
    that a done? Would it 've changed 'em?

Nah. But I'm going back tomorrow. And then I'm gonna be knocking on some fucking gates of me own.
I'll be seeing ya.

SCENE 11
Jeremy Wonfrey's Office
Deborah sits on her own. Jeremy enters.

JEREMY	Debbie... *(tries to touch her.)*
DEBORAH	Don't.
JEREMY	Look. You know me.
DEBORAH	Too bloody well. Don't touch me.
JEREMY	No. I mean. Well you know about my temper. I just can't seem to... well, control it sometimes. I did get a bit carried away. I said things... well, things I shouldn't have said. I'm sorry.
DEBORAH	What about Simon Rillings?
JEREMY	What?
DEBORAH	What are you going to do about his piece?
JEREMY	What do you want me to do?
DEBORAH	I mean it Jeremy. If you don't work out a way to do his piece I'll walk out of the company.
JEREMY	Very well.
DEBORAH	Sorry?
JEREMY	Very well, I'll speak to him.
DEBORAH	You mean it?
JEREMY	Yes.
DEBORAH	Thanks, Jeremy.
JEREMY	OK.
DEBORAH	Come on then.
JEREMY	What?
DEBORAH	Let's go.
JEREMY	Where?

DEBORAH   Let's go to see Simon.

JEREMY   Now?

DEBORAH   Yes. Now. He's very upset. I'm worried about him. Seriously.

JEREMY   Can't we just phone him. Arrange a meeting?

DEBORAH   No. It's not the same. I've just got a feeling we should see him now.

JEREMY   You mean... Go to – that place?

DEBORAH   Eden Estate, yes.

JEREMY   But it's getting late.

DEBORAH   Frightened?

JEREMY   No. Well, yes actually. I thought we might go to my club, not the nether reaches of *Beowulf.*

DEBORAH   Look we need to go now. He's so upset. I'm really concerned about him. It would mean the world to him if you went to see him there.

JEREMY   No. It's not necessary.

DEBORAH   You could see where I grew up.

JEREMY   Look...

DEBORAH   But we must see Simon tonight. Tell him his work is valued here. Put your pride to one side for once. Or I really will walk from this place. Please Jeremy, this is important to me.

JEREMY   Alright...alright. We'll go. But look... I really didn't mean to hurt him. It's just that... This place. You know? It can get to you. One really, in the scheme of world events, means very little. But there's something about being the custodian of these great works and this great art form that... damages you. The power? The works themselves? The intrigue? I don't know. I actually like Simon. I saw the look of fear in his face when I told him his piece had been cancelled. And I felt... such pity. Really. Huge compassion and sympathy but the monster's hand had hold of my heart and I couldn't stop my rage. I knew I was lacerating someone's dream but the obscenity of destroying a young soul – well. It delighted me. The sheer perversion of it was delicious. The look of terror and fragility on his face gave me a kind of – dark happiness. And I'm disgusted at myself for it. I used to feel such – innocent joy when I heard music. It – stupid – but it saved me in a way. Now I wonder what happened to that younger me. Expense accounts and meetings and the sheer joy at the dash and power of it all. So it's not just you, Debbie... I want to talk to him. I really do.

Deborah gets up and holds Jeremy.

DEBORAH   Oh Jeremy. I've never heard you... oh.

JEREMY   Don't tell anyone I said that. *(smiles)* Don't want my Mister Bastard image ruined overnight.

DEBORAH   OK.

JEREMY   Another thing.

DEBORAH   What?

JEREMY   Do we really have to go to this bloody housing estate?

DEBORAH   Yes! Come on.

JEREMY   Oh shit. The things I do for this bloody wretched little art form.

They laugh. Lights fade.

SCENE 12

Mr Rillings' Flat. Music: "Hurdygurdy" from Schubert's "Wintereisse". Lonely. Mournful. Desolate. The lights come up on a solitary figure. It is Simon. He joins in with the mournful singing voice on the tape. Simon is deep within his own "Winter's Journey". He touches a button. The music stops.

He puts another tape in the double-tape deck. This time the music is the insane, desperate optimism of the twenties / thirties recording of "The Sun Has Got His Hat On". Simon listens, remembers something. He turns it down a bit. Takes out the Schubert tape, puts a blank one in, speaks into the microphone of the machine.

SIMON   I forgot to say: Please forgive me. Please. My love for you is like Art. Eternal and infinite.

He then turns off the second tape deck. He turns up "The Sun Has Got His Hat On". He puts his head in the noose we now see in his hand. He puts it round his neck. He stands on a chair.

SIMON   Well. They gave me enough rope. *(dark laugh. Stops)* Dad. I'm sorry. Father. I'm sorry.

He jumps off the chair, twists on the rope. "The Sun Has Got His Hat On" mocks his agony. He twists and convulses, struggles, kicks in agony. He dies.

SCENE 13
Eden Estate. Night. Jeremy is being led through the concrete tower blocks.

JEREMY   Where did you say his flat was?
DEBORAH   It's just along here. Look. That's the chip shop we used to go to.
JEREMY   Right. I think I've seen enough, Debbie.
DEBORAH   Come on. Don't be such a chicken.
JEREMY   What is this all in aid of? Apart from the obvious social anthropology. Let's just find his flat.

DEBORAH   We will. Have a look. That's all. You said you were interested in having a look.

JEREMY   I'm looking. I'm looking.

Velvetblade appears out of the shadows, walks behind them, quietly.

DEBORAH   We're being followed.

JEREMY   Oh my God.

DEBORAH   Don't look round.

VELVETBLADE *Oi! Oi, you!* I know you, don't I? I seen you before, ain't I? I recognise the chick.

JEREMY *(under his breath)* An opera lover? Here?

VELVETBLADE *(goes up to them)* I seen you before, ain't I?

JEREMY   Well I...

VELVETBLADE   Yeah. You was at Eden School, weren't ya?

DEBORAH   Yeah.

VELVETBLADE   You was a few years above us. You ain't half turned out tasty.

DEBORAH   Thank you.

VELVETBLADE   Debbie sumfin', ain't it?

DEBORAH   Yes. I'm amazed you remembered.

VELVETBLADE   Course I do. You remember me?

DEBORAH   Well, not really to be honest.

VELVETBLADE   No. Just a kid, I was. Who's he?

JEREMY   I'm the third person. Pleased to meet you.

VELVETBLADE   Course you bleedin' are, mate. There's only three of us. Who's this third person everyone's talking about these days?

JEREMY   Jeremy.

VELVETBLADE   Spare a few coins, mate?

JEREMY   Well. Oh well. *(roots in his pockets for some coins. Gives them to him)*

VELVETBLADE   Nice one. Whatcha doin' now?

DEBORAH   Well. I'm a singer.

VELVETBLADE   What in clubs 'n pubs 'n that?

JEREMY   Not exactly. Well it's been nice to meet you. We'll be off now.

DEBORAH   No, Jeremy. *(To Velvetblade)* No. I'm an opera singer now. Don't laugh.

VELVETBLADE   I can't laugh 'cos I don't get what you mean. That Country and Western?

DEBORAH   What?

VELVETBLADE   The Grand Ol' Opry. Me Dad's bang into that stuff. Fuckin' hate it meself.

DEBORAH   No, it's –

JEREMY   We'd better be off. Cheerio. *(leads her away)*

DEBORAH   Nice seeing you.

VELVETBLADE   Yeah. *(As they leave, calling after them)* He's your manager. He must be, in that suit. Must be doin' alright, love. Send my regards to Nashville.

Blackout.

SCENE 14

Mr Rillings' Flat. Simon is hanging dead. His father comes in, excited.

RILLINGS   Simon? Simon?

His son swings in silence. The phone rings. Rillings feels for it.

RILLINGS *(on phone)* Hello? Simon...? Ah, Father Collins... How are you...? Yes. I know. It's on any minute now... Course I remembered... I know... Yes. Yes, we're all proud of him. All his aunties are tuning in. I hope he doesn't use any bad language like last time... Yes. Let's go – it's starting. I can't think where he might be... Yes, God Bless You too, Father. *(puts phone down)* Simon? Where are you? Oh well.

He puts on the radio as his son hangs above him. We hear the interview:

INTERVIEWER So, do you think there's room for new work these days?

SIMON   Yeah. Course. I think there's never been a better time for new work.

INTERVIEWER Why do you say that?

SIMON   Well, because there's a new era being born. A new feel in the air. The truth is needed now.

INTERVIEWER But after the critics savaged your string quartet, what gives you such optimism?

RILLINGS   You tell him, son.

SIMON   I can't and won't allow myself to be crippled by the small. I have to go on. I must go on. I won't give in to these people. Beethoven is my hero. He suffered more than I ever did. And, like him, in the end I believe in humanity. I believe in the power of the human voice. That's why my next piece will be sung music theatre.

INTERVIEWER You mean an opera?

SIMON   Yeah. If you insist on calling it that.

INTERVIEWER Why wouldn't you call it that?

SIMON   I wouldn't call it that because it immediately puts most people off. They rightly assume that it will have nothing to say to them. But I believe that it can. I believe that when the power of the human voice meets the power of music meets the power of drama you can have the greatest, most transcendent art of all. *(beat)* My God, it can be fantastic. And that beauty should be controlled by the people. Not just a rich and powerful over-educated yet deeply ignorant few. Ignorant intellectually and spiritually.

INTERVIEWER The people? Do people still say that? Marvellous.

SIMON   Well I do.

INTERVIEWER What do you mean by 'controlled'?

SIMON   It's all about control. The arts in this country at the moment are controlled and restricted by people who have never created a piece of art in their lives. And yet they're the ones who live well. They're the ones that are celebrated. They're the ones that society so richly rewards. And yet they are a plague of deeply venal, corrupt snobs who are more viciously ruthless and crooked than any street corner thug you could ever meet. They are all looking out for each other with a silent nod and a wink. A dinner here, a phone call there. A life ruined here. It's all in a day's work to them. Position, power and a good dinner and to hell with new talent and the art it brings.

INTERVIEWER Might this sound a bit paranoid, perhaps?

SIMON   Yes. It is paranoid. Because to be an artist today is to be paranoid. But you must be as cunning as a snake while remaining as innocent as a dove as The Man said. And keep working. Stay on your toes. Remember who you are and those that love you. And never give in. I will never give in.

INTERVIEWER Well, well. Thank you very much, Simon Rillings.

RILLINGS   Well done, lad. Well done.

He sits under the swinging corpse of his son, smiling proudly. Lights fade.

SCENE 15

Eden Estate. Night. The docks or deserted shopping mall. Jeremy and Deborah walk together.

JEREMY   Come on. Where did we park the bloody car?
We'll drive the rest of the way to his flat.

DEBORAH   It was down the end here. It's all changed so
much.

JEREMY   Yes, well I think we've had enough of your
sentimental journey. You should have brought along a
colour sup journalist.

DEBORAH   Alright.

JEREMY   'I'm still close to my people, says The Workers'
Diva.'

DEBORAH   Alright. That's enough.

JEREMY   I mean I think you've proved your point. I
mean you don't have to lecture me, you know. I voted
Labour.

DEBORAH   I know. Oh look – that's the bus stop where I
kissed Gary Collins for the first time.

JEREMY   Really.

DEBORAH   My first love.

JEREMY   Really.

DEBORAH   He was lovely.

*The gang flash up, lit by a faulty neon. A tableau. They
disappear again.*

JEREMY   What was that?

DEBORAH   It looked like... Come on, let's get out of here.

*The gang flash up again. Totally different place. Neon-lit flash.
They disappear.*

JEREMY   Right. The car. *(starts to run)*

DEBORAH   No. Don't run. It's worse.

They start to walk slowly. The gang slowly walk behind them. They carry a portable sound system.

GIRLY *(a strange whisper)* Lovely. Lovely. Lovely. What have we here? Lovely lovely lovely lovely lovely lovely lovely lovely lovely. And ugly.

Deborah and Jeremy are now confronted by the gang.

JEREMY   Hallo.
SHRIMPDICK   What's hello about it?

Pause. They look at Shrimpdick.

GIRLY   You can only say that if someone says good morning or good evening.
SHRIMPDICK   Sorry, Girly.
GIRLY   Good evening.
DEBORAH   What's good about it?
GIRLY   Very good, gorgeous. Very bleedin' good. Very fuckin' good. Very very very very very very very very very fuckin' good.
JEREMY   Well it's been very nice meeting you. *(starts to lead Deborah off)*
GIRLY *(stops him)* Not so fast, Mr Smell. Mr Cologne, is it? *(sniffs him like an animal)* Mr-I-recognise-that-smell. We done a warehouse full of it last year. *(sniffs him)* Yeah. I know what you smell of. You smell of clean linen. Of articles in magazines. I've read 'em. You smell of a clean, big house. You smell of kids and books and a big car and one hundred per cent woollen designer suits. You smell of acceleration and leather upholstery and university and old humour and aspirin and country weekends and affairs and forgotten private school afternoons and money and lies

and treacle pudding and landscaped gardens and the best birds. You smell of the air you breathe which is the smell of the Gardens of Gethsemane, not of the lonely suffering know-yourself kind, but the high priest arriving to nick-the-holy-man kind. That's what you smell of. Thin, thin air. You stink of all that's gone. Sweet and stale and disgustingly brief.

An Irish Priest on a bicycle comes on and cycles in a big circle round the lads.

PRIEST *(cheerful)* Hello there.
GIRLY   Good evening, Father.
MR SMITH   Good evening, Father.
VELVETBLADE   Good evening, Father.
SHRIMPDICK   Good evening, Father.
PRIEST *(smiling)* Hello there. Hello there. Hello there. Hello there. Hello there.
JEREMY *(calls to priest)* Hey! I think we might be in trouble here.
DEBORAH   Jeremy, don't.

The priest just carries on, circling the boys on his bike.

PRIEST *(like a mantra)* Hello there. Hello there. Hello there. Hello there. Hello there.

He circles them several more times. They all watch him. He finally cycles away. Silence.

GIRLY   He's our mate. We all used to be his altar servers. That was before. Before... the fall. So, you think you might be in some trouble here, do you?

Blackout.

SCENE 16

Mr Rillings' Flat. Rillings sits under the hanging corpse of his son. Hears a noise.

RILLINGS   Simon? Is that you? Simon? *(Silence)* Oh well. *(He goes over to the tape deck, finds a new tape in there)* I told him not to leave tapes in the machine. He knows it confuses me. *(He puts it on)*

SIMON'S VOICE *(on tape. His weak voice is in stark contrast to the confidence of the interview)* Hello Dad. I don't know how to say this to you or why I've done it. But I'm here. Right now. Above you. In more ways than one. I just couldn't take it. It. It. I just couldn't. The pain. The lies of the world I'm in. They've destroyed me, Dad. You see – I don't fit in. I'm sick of any publicity I get starting with: 'Boy from the housing estate makes good'. I hate them and don't belong with them but I don't belong where I started from either. I'm alone, Dad. Apart from you. You were the only source of love I've ever known. You and my music. But it's not just that. It's not just them. There's a sadness in my soul that feels as old as the centre of the earth. And as deep. *(pause)* I'm not strong enough, Dad. But I know there's a Good. I know there's a God. I just hope you and He can forgive me.
I ain't in darkness now, Dad. I will be in light. Please make sure my work is published. Please pray for me. I must believe in the infinite mercy of God. I know I should have continued. What I've done is cowardly and wrong...

(The tape starts again, this time with "Sun has got his hat on" in background.)

I forgot to say: Please forgive me... Please. My love for you is like Art. Eternal and infinite.

We then possibly hear his hanging sounds. Rillings gets up – touching and feeling his way around the flat. He eventually finds the hanging body of his son. He touches it. Feels it. Recognises it. He holds it. No tears. We hear "Wintereisse" fade up as other music fades.

RILLINGS *(quietly)* Just a few of us. The bombing raid ended. We jumped over the side of the ship. It was on fire. Smell of petrol, aviation fluid, gasoline. The sea was on fire. My mate Dave was on fire. His face melted. I couldn't save him. Friends on fire. Screaming and drowning. The ship started to sink. Our home sinking. The Nazis came back, shooting at us in the water. I wanted to die I wanted to go under. I needed to die and rest in the soothing wet flames... I didn't. I lived.

Rillings hugs his dead son as the Schubert plays and the lights fade.

SCENE 17
Eden Estate. Night.
The gang with Jeremy and Deborah.

JEREMY Look. I'd rather be going now.
GIRLY Who's stopping you?
JEREMY Thanks. *(starts to move off with Deborah)*
GIRLY *Oi!* Don't I know you?
JEREMY No.
GIRLY Not you. Her.
VELVETBLADE Yeah. She's the one I told you about. Went to Eden.
GIRLY Yeah. Did ya?
DEBORAH Yeah.
GIRLY When?
DEBORAH I was a few years above you, I think.
GIRLY Saints preserve us, so you were!

VELVETBLADE Saints preserve us, so you were!

MR SMITH   Saints preserve us, so you were!

SHRIMPDICK   Saints preserve us, so you were!

JEREMY   Well, we'll be off then.

GIRLY *(goes over to her)* Saints preserve us, so you were. So – what happened?

DEBORAH   How do you mean?

GIRLY   You know what I mean. Look at ya. Way you dress. You're with him. *Him.* Way you smell.

VELVETBLADE   How she smell, Girly?

MR SMITH   Yeah, give it up, Girly.

SHRIMPDICK   What she smell like Girly?

GIRLY *(goes very, very close to Deborah, smells her. She trembles)* Apples. Fruit. Fear. *(He puts the tape that Rillings gave him into the machine)* The old fella give me this.

Music rises. It is Vivaldi's 'Music for Mandolins'. Baroque. Delicate. Exquisite. Girly preens in front of Deborah. She watches him. He dances weirdly, madly for her. He takes her gently by the hand. They engage in a gallant, courtly-love dance. Then erotic, dark. They move together. Jeremy is devoured with jealousy. Girly and Deborah are locked into each other. Magical. Beautiful. Own world. The lights could exclude the others. They eventually stop. Lights back to previous state. The gang applaud. Jeremy doesn't. Girly goes over to him.

GIRLY   Didn't you like it?

JEREMY   Well...

GIRLY   Well what?

JEREMY   It had a...

GIRLY   What?

JEREMY   A certain quality.

GIRLY   You hated it, didn't ya?

JEREMY   Well...

GIRLY   Why can't you posh cunts say what you fuckin' mean?

SHRIMPDICK   Mean what ya say.

VELVETBLADE   What's he fuckin' saying?

MR SMITH   He looks like a stale bogey you smear on yer headboard.

GIRLY   What did you reckon?

JEREMY   Well there's nothing much to say. Because there was nothing much to see.

MR SMITH   Chin 'im, Girly-boy.

GIRLY   Nah. He's entitled to his opinion. This is a democracy after all, ain't it?

JEREMY   I hope so. No offence though. It just sort of – well... lacked all discipline. I mean – no...

GIRLY   What? Go on.

JEREMY   Well, when one's seen some of the best dance companies in the world...

GIRLY   Yeah?

DEBORAH   Jeremy –

JEREMY   Well, no offence, but your – display just doesn't quite seem to sit well in their company, that's all.

DEBORAH   Jeremy, please –

JEREMY   Yes. Can we go now? We've got an urgent meeting.

GIRLY   It was just a bit of joy. For me. And me mates. And her. *(To Deborah)* You liked it, didn't you?

DEBORAH   Yeah. I did actually. Look – I think we should go now.

GIRLY   But before you do, I'd just like to smell you again *(To Deborah)* D'ya mind?

DEBORAH   No. Go on then.

Girly smells her.

SHRIMPDICK   Go on. Whatchee smell of?

VELVETBLADE   He's dead good at this.

GIRLY   Leaves. Lies. Silk stockings and black hair. Top gear and high heels and sadness. She smells of here but not here. I can smell the council flat but I can smell the velvet curtains too. I can smell the lies she told. To herself. You smell of cocktails and a long list of fruity forgetful fucks. You smell of him and betrayed-by-him sweat-and-glamour-and-showbiz and evil. There's a fragrance. Hold on. There's a fragrance of you. That's it. It's sweet. It's pure. But it's too faint and too distant under all the stink of him and what you've lost and where you've been.

DEBORAH *(congratulates)* That's right! It's a good perfume but you'd think they could find a shorter name for it, wouldn't you?

GIRLY   Humour. She's got a sense of humour. *(suddenly grabs her wrist and forces her to the ground)* Right. Who are you? What are you?

DEBORAH   Debbie Mullins. I'm a singer.

Jeremy tries to intervene, but he is kicked in the groin by Velvetblade.

GIRLY   What kind of singer?

VELVETBLADE   Country and Western, I told you.

GIRLY   Sing 'Stand By Your Man'.[1]

DEBORAH   What?

GIRLY   Sing 'Stand By Your Fucking Man'.

DEBORAH   I can't.

GIRLY   *Sing it! (He twists her arm)*

DEBORAH *(sings hesitantly)*
  "Sometimes it's hard to be a woman,
   Giving all your love to just one man..."

---

[1] 'Stand By Your Man' Music and Lyrics by Tammy Wynette and Billy Sherrill.

She continues for a while.

GIRLY　　No. No. Not bad. But it's missing somefin'.

MR SMITH　　It's the *dum dee dum dee dum* bit.

GIRLY　　What?

SHRIMPDICK　　Yeah. The *dum dee dum dee dum* bit in the middle. *(sings it)* "Sometimes it's hard to be a woman..."

SHRIMPDICK/VELVETBLADE/MR SMITH *(as backing singers. Together)* Dum dee dum dee dum.

GIRLY　　Oh yeah. Oi! You! *(To Jeremy)* You do the *dum dee dum dee dum* bit.

JEREMY　　Now look here...

GIRLY　　*Shut it, fuck-wit!* You do the *dum-dee-dum-dee-fuckin'-dum* bit and you do it fuckin' now. OK. *Go!*

DEBORAH *(sings)* "Sometimes it's hard to be a woman..."

JEREMY *(hesitant)* Dum dee dum dee dum.

DEBORAH *(sings)* "Giving all your love to just one man..."

JEREMY　　Dum dee dum dee dum.

GIRLY　　No! You big wanker. There's no *dum dee dum dee dum* bit after "Giving all your love to just one man".

JEREMY　　Oh.

GIRLY　　You were doing well then you fuckin' ruined it. Didn't 'e, eh? What do our posh twats on the telly panel think a that? What do our distinguished guests on the Arts discussion programme think a that?

VELVETBLADE　　He fuckin' spoilt it.

SHRIMPDICK　　He lost it in the second half, Brian.

MR SMITH　　He murdered it.

VEVETBLADE　　He robbed me, I felt, of the fuckin' joy of the moment.

SHRIMPDICK　　Spoilt a perfectly good tune.

GIRLY　　You hear that? That was their opinion of your performance. Their democratic opinion. My mate has hit the nail on the nail on the nail. You spoilt a perfectly good tune. You-spoilt-a-perfectly-good-tune.

JEREMY We're leaving. *(makes to go)*

Girly slashes Jeremy's face with a razor very, very quickly. He screams.

GIRLY Ain't you got no music in your soul? There's no *dum dee dum dee dum* after "Giving all your love to just one man." *Got it?*

JEREMY *(shock)* Yes. *(holds his face)*

GIRLY *(quiet)* Good. Now. What sort of singer are you really?

DEBORAH Just a singer. Country and Western.

GIRLY Come on. You ain't no Country and Western singer. There's too much soul in it. It's too beautiful. It's too Irish. Like us.

DEBORAH My family's Irish.

GIRLY Yeah? You should be even more ashamed then. What sort of singing, then?

DEBORAH Opera.

GIRLY What?

DEBORAH Opera.

GIRLY What?

DEBORAH Opera.

GIRLY What?

DEBORAH Opera.

GIRLY What?

DEBORAH Opera.

GIRLY What?

DEBORAH *Opera! Opera! Opera!*

GIRLY *(beat)* What?

JEREMY She said opera.

GIRLY What?

JEREMY   Nothing.

GIRLY   *What?*

JEREMY   Opera.

GIRLY   What?

JEREMY   Opera.

VELVETBLADE What?

JEREMY   Opera.

SHRIMPDICK What?

JEREMY   Opera.

MR SMITH   What?

JEREMY   Opera... she sings...

GIRLY   *What? What? What?*

JEREMY   Opera. She's an opera singer.

VELVETBLADE What's that?

GIRLY   Don't show yer fuckin' ignorance. We know what opera is. And we know what it ain't. And it ain't plenty. Go on then. Fuck off the pair of you.

Deborah gets up from the floor. Jeremy helps her.

VELVETBLADE What ya doing?

MR SMITH   We just letting 'em go?

SHRIMPDICK We can't do that.

GIRLY   There's nothing there. Go on. Piss off.

Jeremy's mobile rings.

GIRLY   Answer it, then. *Answer it!*

Jeremy does, nervous in front of them. Then suddenly absorbed in the call.

JEREMY   Hello. Jeremy Wonfrey, yes... yes... Simon
Rillings? Yes... Oh no. When...? Oh my God. Are you
sure...? His father? Oh my God... Yes. Yes I will... Thank
you.

DEBORAH   What, Jeremy?

JEREMY   Let's go. I'll tell you later.

GIRLY   No. Now, Jeremy. What is it? Tell her.

JEREMY   It's Simon Rillings. He's hanged himself.

DEBORAH   Oh my God. Oh God.

JEREMY   I know. Oh no. His father found him. Oh God.
Oh God.

DEBORAH *(puts arm round him)* Let's go.

Girly goes over to Jeremy. He puts his arm round him.

GIRLY   What's the matter?

JEREMY   I could have been more... Simon... I don't
believe it. Oh God, I was too...

DEBORAH   Come on, Jeremy.

JEREMY   If only I'd... if I could have...

GIRLY *(soft)* You know what, Jeremy? It's good to hear that
you care about Simon. Simon Rillings and his dad.

*He slashes Jeremy's other cheek with the razor. Jeremy
screams. He kicks Jeremy on to the floor.*

GIRLY   You are now about to enter the world of your
very worst dreams, Jeremy.

DEBORAH   Stop it. For God's sake.

GIRLY   You are now about to taste the brimstone and
hear the flutter of the wings of the very darkest angel. The
avenging angel.

DEBORAH   You don't realise. We've just had terrible news.
Please let us go now.

GIRLY   Debbie Mullins. I recognise the name now. What happened to you, Debbie? What happened? Think you'd pay us a nostalgic visit, did you Debs? Have a look at the old days. A trip down memory lane.

VELVETBLADE Welcome home, Debs.

MR SMITH   Welcome back, babes.

SHRIMPDICK Welcome back to the land of the real dicks.

GIRLY   Course I know who you are. But do you? Why you here?

DEBORAH   I was just showing my friend round here. I grew up round here. Went to school round here. I should have known...

GIRLY   What should you have known?

DEBORAH   That I wouldn't... That I couldn't...

GIRLY   Wouldn't? Couldn't?

VELVETBLADE Sounds like another fuckin' Country and Western song.

DEBORAH   I don't know why I felt I could... Please just let us go now. It was stupid of me to try. To try to return... Just get on with being shut out... both worlds... Why did I ever want your approval? I don't need anyone's approval. Yours or theirs. Both brutal bunches of bastards. I should have known that you couldn't... wouldn't.

MR SMITH   There she goes again.

DEBORAH   Simon... Simon. Oh God. Simon.

GIRLY   Now. To the business in hand. *(To Jeremy)* You are charged that a young man, one of our own... Yeah. Too fuckin' right. One of us... Came to you with a brilliant new opera. Yes. O-p-era. Remember what Father Reilly taught us. Latin classes. And you shat on him. He came to you with hope in his heart, with God in his soul and you destroyed him. You have sinned. "Through your fault, your fault, your most grievous fault." His blind dad. Think what he's going through now. Blind justice. That's what we want. Get his fuckin' trousers off!

The gang eagerly pull Jeremy's trousers off. They hold him tight.

GIRLY   So this is what happened. This young artist of our own goes to this bleedin' piece of posh to get a gig and to large it for this bird Debbie, he knocks him back.

VELVETBLADE   How d'ya know all this, Girly?

GIRLY   The old blind man you wanted to razor. That was his Old Man.

MR SMITH   Nah. Never. We wouldn't do that.

GIRLY   Oh yes you fuckin' would. Not deliberate. But you woulda done it. Now you have a chance to do justice instead. I went back with the old geezer and I met this Simon Rillings. And now he's topped hisself 'cos of this shite being snide to the geezer to impress this bird. *(He rolls Jeremy's sleeve up. Jeremy struggles but the gang hold him)* You will now experience your just deserts. The desert of your fuckin' soul. The death of a thousand cuts. *(gets out his razor followed by the gang)* But first. What can you say in your defence?

JEREMY   Please. Look. I'm sorry. I really am. I can't quite take in what's happened. He was a depressive sort of person.

GIRLY   So why weren't you fairer with him then?

JEREMY   Yes. Exactly. Why?

Girly slashes Jeremy's arm. Followed by a slash each from the gang. Jeremy screams.

GIRLY   That's just a taste, my evil friend. A taste of the punishment you will receive on your long, dark night of the soul.

JEREMY   What right have you to judge me?

GIRLY   Every right. Every fuckin' right, OK?

JEREMY   Look, I'm really sorry about what happened to him.

The gang hold him down. One holds Deborah back. Girly slashes Jeremy's feet with the razor.

GIRLY   Good. I'm glad. 'Cos it'll make your pain more – exquisite.

SHRIMPDICK I love that drink.

VELVETBLADE What?

SHRIMPDICK Especially chocolate flavour.

MR SMITH What bleedin' drink's that?

SHRIMPDICK Milk drink. Chocolate Exquisite.

VELVETBLADE That's *Nesquick,* you cunt.

MR SMITH Yeah. I love *Nesquick.* Shame they never done sausage and mash flavoured *Nesquick.*

VELVETBLADE I thought that was the only fuckin' flavour they done.

GIRLY   Don't lower the tone. You see, Jeremy, I'm doin' this for a reason. Don't take no comfort in the fact that this is some random stylee violent vibe. This is 'cos you done wrong. Big time harm. And you gotta pay for it. You see what I'm saying, geezer? *(He slashes Jeremy's other foot)*

JEREMY *(screams in pain)* Please. For God's sake.

GIRLY   For God's sake. Really?

DEBORAH   Please let us go. Just let us go now. Please.

GIRLY   Look. I can't do that.

MR SMITH Or banana flavour.

VELVETBLADE My mate once made a frog flavour milk shake.

SHRIMPDICK Ugh. How?

VELVETBLADE Put it in his mum's blender.

SHRIMPDICK Was it live?

VELVETBLADE Yeah.

SHRIMPDICK What? He put a live frog in his mum's blender?

VELVETBLADE Yeah.

SHRIMPDICK Ugh. That's horrible. There's no fuckin' call for that. That's just fuckin' cruel, that is.

MR SMITH Yeah. Senseless fuckin' cruelty.

SHRIMPDICK Mindless fuckin' violence, that is.

VELVETBLADE Yeah. You're right. But that's boys for ya.

SHRIMPDICK/VELVETBLADE Yeah.

GIRLY   Shut it you lot. Look. I can't let you go, Jeremy. It's my – responsibility. I gotta do this. Think of the pain I'll be saving you later.

JEREMY   What?

GIRLY   In Hell. I'm saving you a lot of pain when you get to the next life.

DEBORAH You sadistic fuckin' nutcase.

GIRLY   Don't you fuckin' say that to me. *(slashes Jeremy's leg. He screams)* Don't fuckin' put it down to that. I mean this. I'm fuckin'... aware of it. I ain't no fuckin' nutcase. I'm aware of the service I'm doing this fucker. I'm fully fuckin' aware of the peril I'm putting my soul in. Demonic teacher. To save this bastard. *(beat)*

SHRIMPDICK What'd it taste like?

VELVETBLADE What?

SHRIMPDICK The frog-milk-shake.

VELVETBLADE I don't fuckin' know do I, you moron. Dya think I was gonna drink a fuckin' frog fuckin' milk shake? *(beat)*

MR SMITH I've had vole.

SHRIMPDICK Do what?

MR SMITH I've had vole milk shake.

SHRIMPDICK You fuckin' liar.

VELVETBLADE No one's had vole milk shake.

MR SMITH   I have. Same thing. Blender job.

VELVETBLADE   Alright. What'd it taste like then?

MR SMITH   Unusual really. Sort of nutty, woody, with a trace of smoke and yet with a certain –

SHRIMPDICK   You tossy liar, you know what I mean?

MR SMITH   I ain't. There's no taste quite like vole.

VELVETBLADE   Oh shut it will ya or I'll put your knob in a blender.

MR SMITH   Look if you had a choice of my Keeley's cooking or a glass of vole milkshake you'd be going, "Gimme the vole, gimme the vole."

GIRLY   That's enough. We got work to do here. Now lie back mate. Go with it. I'd advise it. *Tu es culpa. Tu es maxima culpa.* And you have to pay. It's better to do it here on this earth than in the next. *(He puts on the Vivaldi Mandolin Music, starts to slice Jeremy's legs with the razor. He does it in a clinical, removed yet artistic way. Trance-like by the music. Jeremy screams with pain. Two of the gang hold him down. Deborah tries to stop them but is held back by the third gang member. He works his way up Jeremy's legs. Thin, deep cuts. To Jeremy)* What do you think of the performance? The music? I'm sure you've heard it played better before. *(slash)* Is it as good as Simon Rilling's music? *(slash)* Why did you hate his opera so much? *(slash)* You gave him so much pain, he went and hung himself. Alone and fuckin' terrified. *(slash)* What is it about people like you? *(slash)* What are you? Who are you? From what fuckin' planet of cruelty do you all come from? *(slash)* Because as much as this hurts, it doesn't hurt as much as the hurt you caused that tortured little geezer. *(slash)* Feel the pain, Jeremy. Feel the pain. *(slash. He shouts)* Feel the fuckin' pain! Feel the pain! Feel the pain! Feel the pain! Feel the pain! Feel the pain! Feel the pain! Feel the pain! Feel the pain! *(beat. Then quiet)* It's your only chance of salvation.

Lights fade.

Spotlight on Deborah.

DEBORAH   It's like I've always been here. Silent, little, trapped. Fucking violent bastards. We know what boys are like. We know what dads are like. We know what his beatings are like. Were like. Are like. Beatings. Cruelty. Semen. My voice fills with the genius of Mozart's mind. Mozart's soul. It passes through me through labial vibrations real muscle real tendons real hurt and real pain. The mystical genius from air and mind and soul vibrating in the flesh of my throat to bring sublime heaven to this earth. All too human. All too fucking human. The laughs. The jokes in the green room. The displacement banter. Fart joke here. Sex gag there. Anything to take us away from the dark fucking danger of soul to soul contact. Knowing that up there in front of them in the dark, we'll be playing midwife to the genius of music; to go from a soul's abstract idea through the conduit of real flesh and muscle and blood into the gristle of strangers' ears and flying back to abstract thought and into souls again. The miracle. And the cruelty. The cruelty of the people who make this. Who allow you to make it. They don't do it themselves but they have the power to stop you doing your God-given duty. It's art for god's sake. What we do has some – meaning. Human. All too human. All too unworthy. *(beat)*

A terrible scream pierces the darkness. Lights snap back to previous state and the Mandolin Music.

JEREMY   *Please stop!*
GIRLY   Oh yes, Jeremy. It'll all be over soon.

He now slashes Jeremy's upper body. His body is now extremely lacerated and bloody. Mr Smith takes a tin out of his jacket. He starts to sprinkle liquid from it over Jeremy's body.

GIRLY   Lighter fuel! Good!
MR SMITH   Yeah. Torch the cunt.
VELVETBLADE Torch the toff!

They dance round Jeremy who is screaming in terror and pain.

GIRLY   Think of it as a purification, Jeremy.
DEBORAH   Please. Please stop it.

A shaft of white light beams across the stage. The other lights dim. A storm wind begins to blow. Rillings appears. He is carrying the body of his dead son through the streets. He looks like an Old Testament prophet or a William Blake drawing. His white hair blows in the wind. The gang and Deborah watch in silence.

RILLINGS *(quotes from the Psalms)*
   "Come back God, rescue my soul
   Save me if you love me
   For in death there is no remembrance of You
   Who can sing your praises in Sheol?"

He slowly carries his dead son across the stage. As he approaches the group, the lights go slowly back to the previous state. The wind begins to drop in volume.

JEREMY   Help! Please! Help me. They're going to kill me.
RILLINGS *(stops)* Kill?

Girly runs over to Rillings.

GIRLY   Hello mate. Come on. Let me help ya.
RILLINGS   You? The lad who helped me before?
GIRLY   Yeah.

Girly helps Rillings to rest the body on the floor. Rillings sinks to his knees, abject over his son, cradling him on the floor.

RILLINGS   You talked to Simon.
GIRLY   Fuckin' 'ell mate, I'm sorry.
RILLINGS   What are you up to?
GIRLY   We're executing someone.
RILLINGS   No.
GIRLY   We have to.
RILLINGS   *No!*
GIRLY   What?
RILLINGS   For God's sake. Look what they did to my son.
  Have you no respect?
GIRLY   Yeah. That's why we're doing it.

He lights the lighter, goes over to Jeremy. Holds lighter inches from his body. About to ignite the fuel.

RILLINGS   If you don't show him mercy, you'll wipe out
  any good you did for me.

Girly stops but keeps flame going.

GIRLY   But you don't know who he is. What he's done.
RILLINGS   Nor do you. You don't know what brought him
  here.
GIRLY   Oh I do. I know alright.
RILLINGS   Whatever he's done, you must stop the wheel.
  Stop the wheel of hate turning. Too much death. Too much
  blindness. Too much rage. You spin the wheel round and
  round until it'll crush this little sad planet of ours. I've seen
  death before. Stop it before you tie yourself to it and it
  crushes you.

GIRLY   *This is the man that killed your son.*
RILLINGS   What?
JEREMY   Oh my God.
GIRLY   This is Jeremy. The geezer that knocked your
    Simon back.

*Rillings walks over slowly to Jeremy on floor. He finds his face.
Touches it.*

RILLINGS   Are you Jeremy Wonfrey?
JEREMY   Yes. Oh my God. Yes. I'm so sorry.

*Rillings emits a scream from the soul. Full of rage and pain. He
goes back to his son, holding him. Girly keeps the lighter flame
going.*

RILLINGS   You. You hurt Simon. More than you can know.
    He's here. And you're alive. Well, that's it boys. Punish him.
    Why should he be allowed to live? The little boy. The sleep-
    less nights. The first football. The prayers. The fights. I'm
    sorry Simon. All those years of care and this is what you've
    done to him.
JEREMY   I'm so sorry. Please...
GIRLY   Look. My lads 'll take you and Simon home. You
    shouldn't be out on the street like this. I'll carry on. I'll deal
    with this.
RILLINGS   No. What am I saying? No. You must let him
    go. For your own sake. And for his. Stop the wheel.
GIRLY   How can you say that? What about justice?
    What about some fuckin' vengeance for Simon? They're
    always getting away with it. They've got to be fuckin' dealt
    with. Your son... Your son was a fuckin' artist. We've got to
    make him pay for his death.

RILLINGS   Young man. Young. Man. I'm touched by your concern. Young. Man. But I'm saving you. I'm saving you from the dreams. The dreams of others dying while you live. The curse of surviving. You know you have to let him go. You know you do.

Pause. Girly turns lighter off. Puts blade away. Walks away slowly, reluctantly. The Gang follow him. They could stand staring from the shadows. Deborah runs to Jeremy, holds him, gets out phone.

DEBORAH *(on phone)* Ambulance. Valley House. Eden Estate. Quick as you can...
RILLINGS   Are they coming?
DEBORAH   Yeah.

Pause

DEBORAH *(To Rillings)* I'm sorry about Simon. I'm so sorry.
RILLINGS   Who's this?
DEBORAH   My name's Debbie. Debbie Mullins.
RILLINGS   Debbie Mullins? Really? Simon was so thrilled you were going to sing his work.
DEBORAH   Yeh. Me too.
RILLINGS   You still will, won't you?
DEBORAH   Well...
RILLINGS   Please sing his songs Debbie Mullins.
DEBORAH   Sing?
RILLINGS   Please...

Pause.

DEBORAH   I'll try...

The lights fade to black, apart from an area of light on Simon's body and Deborah.

DEBORAH   I will try.

The light fades.

The End.

JONATHAN MOORE

PLAYS:

Sea Change	Falmouth Arts Centre, Cornwall.
Obstruct the doors, cause delay and be Dangerous...	
	Cockpit Theatre, London
Street Captives	Edinburgh Festival, Manchester Royal Exchange, Gate Theatre, London.
Treatment	Edinburgh Festival, Gate Theatre, Donmar Warehouse, BBC Film.
Behind Heaven	Manchester Royal Exchange, Donmar.
The Hooligan Nights	National Theatre commission.
This Other Eden	Soho Theatre Company, London
Regeneration	Half Moon Theatre, London
Fall From Light	Manchester Royal Exchange commission.

MUSIC THEATRE TEXTS/LIBRETTI:

Greek (adapted from play by Steven Berkoff) Munich Biennale, Edinburgh Festival, ENO, BBC TV and Radio.

Horse Opera	Channel 4 TV Film.
East and West	Almeida Theatre, London

Mottke The Thief (adapted from novel by Schalom Asch) Bonn Opera

DIRECTING includes:

World Premieres of:

Street Captives	Edinburgh Festival, Gate Theatre
Treatment	Edinburgh Festival, Gate Theatre
Greek	Munich Biennale, Edinburgh Festival.

(Music: Mark Anthony Turnage / Text Steven Berkoff) English National Opera and BBC TV Film (film co-directed with Peter Maniura)

63 Dream Palace	Munich Biennale, German TV.

(Music: Hans Jurgen Von Bose)

Baa Baa Black Sheep   Opera North, Cheltenham Festival.
(Music: Michael Berkeley / Text: David Malouf) BBC TV

Life With An Idiot   English National Opera, Scottish Opera
(Music: Schnittke / Text: Erofeyev)

East and West   Almeida Theatre, London
(Music: Ian McQueen / Text: Moore)

Elegy for Young Lovers   La Fenice, Venice
(Music: Henze / Text: W.H. Auden and Kallman)

Inez de Castro Scottish Opera, Edinburgh Int. Festival
(Music: James MacMillan / Text: Clifford) Oporto 2001 Fest, BBC TV

Mottke the Thief   Bonn Opera
(Music: Bernd Franke / Text: Moore, after novel by Schalom Asch)

Inkle and Yarico   Holders Easter Season, Barbados
(Music: R. Panufnik after Arnold / Text: Coleman)

Cask of Amontillado   Holders, Barbados
(Music: Stewart Copeland)

Facing Goya   Santiago del Compostella, Perrelada Fest,
(Music: Michael Nyman / Text: Hardie) Teatro Principal Valencia

Die Versicherung   State Theatre, Darmstadt
(Music: Jan Muller-Wieland / Text: Peter Weiss)

AWARDS AND NOMINATIONS

Royal Philharmonic Society Award Best Film, *Greek,* BBC TV

Edinburgh Festival   Fringe First Award, *Treatment*

Best Director Award   Munich Biennale, *63: Dream Palace*

Best Librettto Award   Munich Biennale, *Greek*

Olivier Award Nomination   English National Opera, *Greek*

Runner-Up Verity Bargate Award, *This Other Eden,* Soho Theatre Co.

aurora metro press

Founded in 1989 to publish and promote new writing, the press has specialised in new drama and fiction, winning recognition and awards from the industry.

Young Blood, five plays for young performers.
ed. Sally Goldsworthy **ISBN 0-9515877-6-5 £9.95**

Charles Way: Plays for Young People
ISBN 0-9536757-1-8 £9.95

Black and Asian Plays Anthology, introduced by Afia Nkrumah **ISBN 0-9536757-4-2 £9.95**

Six Plays by Black and Asian Women Writers. ed. Kadija George **ISBN 0-9515877-2-2 £7.50**

Best of the Fest. new plays celebrating 10 years of London New Play Festival ed. Phil Setren **ISBN 0-9515877-8-1 £12.99**

Seven plays by women, female voices, fighting lives.
ed. Cheryl Robson **ISBN 0-9515877-1-4 £5.95**

European drama anthologies
Balkan Plots, plays from Central and Eastern Europe, introduced by Gina Landor **ISBN 0-9536757-3-4 £9.95**

Eastern Promise, 7 plays from Central and Eastern Europe eds. Sian Evans and Cheryl Robson **ISBN 0-9515877-9-X £11.99**

Mediterranean plays by women. ed. Marion Baraitser **ISBN 0-9515877-3-0 £9.95**

A touch of the Dutch: plays by women. ed. Cheryl Robson **ISBN 0-9515877-7-3 £9.95**